THE COMPLETE MONEYMAKING MAIL ORDER BUSINESS

D0871691

OWY

THE COMPLETE MONEYMAKING MAIL ORDER BUSINESS

Starting a Successful Mail Order Business with No Money

Donny Lowy

To order additional copies of this book, contact:
Xlibris Corporation
1-888-7-XLIBRIS
www.Xlibris.com
Orders@Xlibris.com

CONTENTS

LOWY

PREFACE

This publication is designed to provide accurate and authoritative information in regard to the subject matter covered. It is sold with the understanding that the author is not engaged in rendering legal, accounting, or other professional service. If legal advice or other expert assistance is required, the services of a competent professional person should be sought.

INTRODUCTION

The success of a business depends on two critical factors that are interrelated. The business needs to be able to reduce its expenses while increasing its revenues. If the manager of the business is successful in growing the business without resorting to a high increase in expenses the business will prosper. This is true as long as the revenues translate into profits after all expenses have been accounted for. To summarize this important principle, the business needs to always ensure, regardless of its development stage, that the revenues should be higher than the expenses. In this case the business will be profitable and will be able to operate independently from any need for outside funding. Many businesses first run into trouble when they have to resort to taking out loans to finance payroll or rent expenses. Their profit margins could be healthy but the financial obligation to pay back the compounding interest will slowly decrease the profit margin as time goes on.

To avoid the necessity for taking out loans you need to be situated in a business that can grow rapidly without requiring a sizable outlay of money. Many retail stores break this rule because their business is seasonable while the high rents they must pay are monthly. The landlord will still demand his rent checks while the retail store is going through a slow seasonal period. The businesses that do manage to operate without having to resort to outside funding are the one's that have very low expenses in comparison towards their revenues. These businesses can afford to have slow periods since the profit they generate in a month period can cover their expenses for the year.

The business that exemplifies this principal is the Mail Order business. The Mail Order business fits this category since the expenses to run it are minimal while the potential profits are exceedingly great. In Mail Order you have the opportunity to eliminate all expenses while producing outstanding profits. The ability to create a high level income without having to spend a great deal of money is due to the nature of the business. The Mail Order business allows you to base your operations from any place you decide. The freedom to locate it anywhere you want enables you to run it from a spare garage, bedroom, dining room, or a small office. Since in many cases you never take possession of the merchandise you do not even need to working space for your business. You only need a mailing address to which your customers can send their payments.

The second advantage of the Mail Order Business is that it can produce unlimited profits for the smart operator. The business can sell merchandise that is inexpensive, or easily reproduced. You can sell anything in Mail Order for which there is a market at the retail level. This includes books, compact discs, videos, electronics, clothing, food and many others items. Your profits from selling these items through the mail are very high since you do not have to pay for rent, labor, advertising and even shipping in many situations. You can also choose to produce your own unique merchandise and sell it for many times what it cost you to produce. Because of the uniqueness of the merchandise customers cannot buy it from another source. If you market it well enough and convince the customers of its high value you will have an easy time selling it for the price you want.

The opportunity to amass wealth in Mail Order is magnificent because you are I most cases committing a very small amount of money to your business while you set yourself up to reap tremendous profits in a very short time. This book can teach you the lucrative methods that have allowed many entrepreneurs with little experience to become millionaires in their own business. Take your time reading this book and applying the information presented to your own needs. You can either decide to start one of the Mail Order Businesses that the book discusses or you can apply the moneymaking strategies in the book to your own enterprise.

CHAPTER 1

Stand Out From The Crowd

The Mail Order business offers allot of opportunities to the enterprising entrepreneur who is willing to put in the time and effort. There are 250,000,000 people in this country alone who have need for products on a daily basis. You have the opportunity to reach every single person in this country by either advertising to his or her parents, spouses, relatives, or friends. If one out of five people in this country decided to act on your offer you could be rest assured that every person in this country would be exposed to your product or service. This means that if you decide to push your business to the maximum there are 250 million prospects in the United States alone for your offer. But the challenge is that there are also thousands of other Mail Order businesses competing for the same prospects. There are other entrepreneurs who will pick up other Mail Order books and attempt to start their own businesses. So how do you compete with them?

I am confident that this book provides more detailed strategic information than any other Mail Order book. If you read this book with an open mind and decide to act on it you will be miles ahead of your competition. I can even teach you ways so you will have no competition. The first step to achieving your ability to compete will the other Mail Order businesses is by realizing that there is enough business out there for everyone to make money. Look at the number of catalogs that arrive in the mail every week and then look at the number of households that receive different catalogs than their neighbors do. This means that each catalog is being

mailed out to customers who might not be receiving another catalog. And even if they are receiving another catalog at the same they
have the option of ordering from both of the catalogs they receive.
You can decide to send them the third catalog that the family will
order from. In reality there are thousands of catalogs being sent
out every week to people who place orders from thousands of catalogs every week. You can join this group and claim your share of
the profits that are being made in Mail Order. I will later teach
you how to claim your share of the millions of dollars that are
being made using catalogs.

For now we will focus on our desire to stand out from the
crowd. There are methods that can be used to differentiate your
business from all other businesses so you can capture more orders
from people than any of your competitors. These methods are based
on human behavior qualities that many experienced Mail Order
experts use to build million dollar businesses. The methods are
based on the knowledge that in order to sell something we need to
be fulfilling the need of the buyer. A person has various needs that
he seeks to fulfill. Those needs are based on the desire for safety,
companionship, money, and social standing. Your Mail Order
business can stand out from the crowd if you tailor your business
to fulfilling the needs of people. Instead of selling a product remember that you are selling the ability to fulfill a personal need.
The best example of this is the sale of a hammer. No one is interested in the intrinsic qualities of a hammer. What people care about
is the ability of the hammer to help them build a home, put a nail
into a hammer, or assemble a piece of furniture. You could sell a
hammer successfully if you pointed out its ability to do put any
nail through the wall. You would be mistaken if you stressed the
shape of the hammer instead of its use for its owner.

A sweater is sold the same way. Instead of spending time de-
scribing the intricate details of the sweater, the successful Mail
Order operator would tell advertise the attractiveness of the sweater.
The advertisement would point out that the sweater provides the
outmost level of warmth while being highly attractive looking.

This way the prospect realizes that two of his needs will be fulfilled. He will look great and attract the opposite sex when he wears the sweater, and he will also be able to keep warm in the harshest winter. The sweater is only a piece of clothing that by itself has little value. But once you convey all the needs that it can fulfill people will be eager to pay any price to have it. Car companies use this strategy when selling high priced cars. They know that any consumer could buy a lower priced car and save $10,000 in the process. But they convince us to buy the higher priced cars by telling us how the car will make us happier, make us look better, and gain us a higher social standing. You can verify how effective this approach is by looking at how many $30,000 cars are on the roads today. I am sure that you can agree with me that cars priced for $20,000 provide the same function as the more expensive models. But the car manufacturers know their business. If they want to sell the higher priced models all they have to do is show consumers how their needs will be met by purchasing their vehicles.

Most Mail Order novices make the mistake of trying to sell their products or services. You can quickly surpass them if instead of focusing on your product you focus on the needs that it fulfills. You should use this effective strategy by applying it to your Mail Order business. Once you learn how to master this method your business will stand out and rapidly move to the head of the line. The key to the method is always asking yourself what need does your product fulfill. Not why someone would like your product, but why would someone use your product. Once you know why someone would use your product you should sell it based on its usage. The basic principle can be summarized by the phrase "People do not buy products, they fulfill needs".

CHAPTER 2

Importance Of Record Keeping

Organization is intrinsic to the ongoing welfare of your Mail Order business. As your business grows you will become swamped with orders from products. You need to take special care to set up a system that you can use to keep track of all of your orders. The system needs to provide you with an easy way to track your expenses, incoming orders, and delivered orders. You need to have a list of your expenses so you can deduct them when it comes time to paying your taxes. The IRS offers many opportunities for the self-employed to reduce their tax liability. All business expenses can be deducted as long as you have proof of the expense and can show that the expense was part of running the business. To keep track of your expense you will need a notebook in which you can write down the day you spent the money, the purposes and a short description of what the expense was for. At the bottom of the page you should staple the recite so you do not loose it.

Keeping track of the orders is just as important. Your customers will expect their orders to be sent out to them promptly. You need to have a list of whom you need to send out products to and which products go with which order. As your business grows you can reach a point where you are receiving thousands of orders a week. If you do not have a system in place you will become swamped with work and fall behind the orders. Another advantage of keeping a list of your customers along with what they ordered is so you can tailor follow up orders to their personal needs. For example, if a customer order a martial arts movie from you he will more than likely want to buy another one in the near future. If you save his name along with a short description of his preferences you can send him a follow up letter offering a list of more martial arts movies that you available. Your established customers are your best source of repeat sales so you want to have system in which you can take advantage of their past purchases.

As your Mail Order business grows you can outsource your record keeping. This means that you can pay someone to set up a system to keep track of your orders and expenses. They can design an easy to use software package that only needs you to input the selected data and the software produces your records.

There are also firms that will fulfill your orders for you, meaning that they will process the orders and send out the merchandise. Some firms will only process the orders and ask you to mail out the merchandise. The advantage of using these firms is that they can keep track of your orders, process credit card payments, send out the orders, and act as your customer service. If you use a full service order fulfillment firm all you need to do is advertise the product and supply the fulfillment firm with merchandise that they can ship out.

There are many approaches that allow you not to have to personally keep track of all of your transactions. You can use them as long as at the end of the year you can still have a clear idea of how much money you brought in and how much you spent. A good accountant will use your records to determine the amount of tax you owed. I am a firm believer in delegating work to outside parties so you can focus on expanding your business instead of wasting your time doing paperwork.

CHAPTER 3

Insist On Payment Along With The Order

Your level of profits depends on the number of sales you are paid for. Many Mail Order companies run into trouble when they ship out merchandise for which they are not paid for. They are hoping that they will encourage customers to place an order if the customer has a 30-day grace period to pay for the merchandise. This strategy can attract a large number of orders from reluctant buyers. But the problem is that along with all the honest buyers who decide to order the product many others will not pay for it. They do not pay because they are unhappy with the order and they do not want to bother having to send it back. So the company that mailed out the order is now stuck with having sent out an order that cost it money for which it will not be reimbursed. Sure, the company can hire a collection agency. But even if the collection agency is able to recover payment for the merchandise the agency will keep half of the payment as its fee. Another problem could arise when a kid places an order for merchandise. The parents might not responsible for paying for it because the child is under 18 and he cannot sign a contract. The agreement to pay for the merchandise in 30-days is null since he was not 18 at the time he signed it. Once again the company has lost the money it spent shipping and producing the merchandise.

You can avoid this dilemma if you insist that the merchandise should be paid for at the time the order is placed. Your advertisement or catalog should contain a form that indicates the need for prepayment of the order. If you are selling through the use of a classified advertisement indicate at the bottom that the buyer should send X amount of dollars along with their order.

Serious buyers will have no problem sending payment ahead of time to you if you convey the feeling of trust. The same that you would have no problem trusting an established catalog such as Fingerhut, you need to establish trust in the eyes of your targeted market. You are establishing this trust so you can ask for payment with your order. The advantage in asking for payment with the order is that you minimize your risk and establish a profit as soon as the order is received. You can then go and spend the money to buy and ship out the product knowing that you have already been paid. Another advantage is that the profit you deposit can start earning interest from the moment you deposit it. If you have to wait another 30 days to receive your money you will have missed out on 30 days of interest earnings. The interest that you earn on your profits can add thousands of dollars to your bottom line when you are dealing with thousands of orders. You can even use the profit to invest in stocks and obtain a higher rate of return than if you had to wait another 30 days to invest it. In order to take advantage of this opportunity you need to demand that you are paid at the time the order is placed. When you become a million dollar operation you might decide to be more aggressive and allow some of your customers to pay after receiving their orders. You can afford to take the chance when your business has grown to the level in which you can afford if 10% of your orders are not paid for. I would suggest holding off offering delayed payment plans until you are selling over a million dollar worth of products each year. Hopefully at this point you will have set aside a very large cushion to cover any small orders that are not paid for.

This is a fantastic business in which you can make hundreds of thousands of dollars a year. The money is great since there are proven techniques used to augment the results your Mail Order business can produce. Stick to them and you will soon be sitting on a very profitable business. Be firm and honest and your customers will respect you and respond by dealing honestly with you.

CHAPTER 4

Promptness Leads To Reorders

People respect when they are treated well. You can grow a profitable Mail Order business if you treat your customers as well as you can. If your costumers are impressed by your service they will recommend you to all of their friends and relatives. You will then have your customers working as sales men for your business. Word of mouth is one of the most effective marketing tools a new business can benefit from. Since people trust their relatives and friends they will follow their advice. They could see your advertisement and still be reluctant to place an order. But if their family tells them that they are really happy with the services they obtained from the company they will then be encouraged to place an order. If you want to take advantage of the benefits that word of mouth advertising can offer you fist have to give people a reason to talk about you. Give them the reason by surpassing their expectations. If they expect to receive the ordered products in two weeks, make sure that it arrives at their homes in one week. If they are expecting their order to arrive in a simple box, wrap it up in fancy gift-wrap paper. Your cost will only be a few cents higher and you will have made a customer for life. Imagine how excited the customer will be when he receives an order expertly packed three days after he placed the order. He will tell his friends how he was not expecting the order to arrive for another two weeks and it already arrived. His friends will be just as impressed and will most likely place an order with you.

The key to impressing your customers is to be prompt and courteous. Ship out their orders as soon as their payments have cleared. Make sure not to delay the order so you can keep your customers happy. In the even that an order will be late for some external reason contact your customer. Let your customer know what the situation is and offer him a 5% discount on his next order for his inconvenience. People understand that things sometimes go wrong and are usually forgiving as long as people are upfront with them. The extra 5% discount is the sweetener that will help him forget that the order is late. The added advantage of offering a 5% discount is that in order for him to utilize it he has to place another order.

The higher level of service that you offer will also have an impact on your level of repeat business. Customers who order from you and are impressed with your services will be more likely to re order from you again. Some people base a majority of their business from re orders. Once you develop a large number of customers who re order you will not have to spend as much money seeking new business. The steady flow of orders from your existing customers could easily be enough to help you retire. The key is to satisfy your customers so they will want to reorder form you and encourage their friends and family's to become customers.

CHAPTER 5

Orders Must Be Shipped Out Within 30-Days

The reputation of your Mail Order business is a big part of what will determine the intensity of success that you achieve. Your reputation will be created as you conduct business and interact with your customers, even if this interaction never becomes personal. People have high expectations for a Mail Order business and you can easily meet those expectations. Once you meet those expectations you will be on your way to developing a loyal base of lifetime customers. Lifetime customers are your most precious assets, since they will place repeat orders for as long as you can supply products that they enjoy. Customers expect to have products delivered to them in a reasonable time. But in addition to their expectations there are laws that regulate the industry. The laws stipulate that you must be able to ship out the product within 30 days. You can offer to deliver the product in a shorter time if you can reasonable be sure that you are able to deliver in that time period.

In the event that you cannot deliver a product in the stated time let the customer know that the product has been delayed but it will be shortly be mailed out. You must have the customers consent to deliver the product after the agreed delivery period. Calling the customer or sending him an email can be a good way to attain consent. You can immediately send him a letter but this might anger the customer since it will take another week for the letter to arrive and for him to reply. I would suggest calling him up and explaining the situation to him. Tell him that while you told him that you would mail out the product within 3 days you are experiencing a very high volume of orders and his product will be out within another 5 days. This way the customer knows that you did not mislead him and that someone is interested in making sure his needs are taken care of.

The 30-day rule for Mail Order is that all orders must be shipped out within 30-days without an exception. In the situation that you cannot mail it out within 30-days you must contact the customer and offer him a full refund. You can ask the customer for permission to ship his order at a later date as long as he understands that he can obtain a full refund if he desires.

The 30-day period begins a soon as the order is received. The order must contain everything that you asked to be included. If you asked for payment then the payment must be included. The 30-day period does not allow time for the check to clear before sending out the order. If you plan on waiting for the check to clear before you send out an order make sure that you will have enough time to ship out the order within 30-days even if you wait for the check to clear. If the check bounces or there is a problem with the order you can wait until the problem is resolved. Once the problem is resolved and the order is considered complete you then have 30 days to ship it out.

CHAPTER 6

Order Fulfillment

To make as much money as possible you want to impress your customers with your shipping and packaging of their orders. But since we know that we need to minimize expenses to increase our profits we must do it carefully so we can reduce the cost of fulfilling the orders. There are basic elements to every order that you want to follow to impress your customers. If you use a drop shipper he will be the one fulfilling your orders so you can avoid having to be concerned with the packaging and shipping of your orders. We will discuss later how you can exponentially grow the size of your product offerings by using drop shippers. Drop shippers supply the products and mail them directly to your customers. You only need to solicit the orders and pass them on to the drop shippers. There will also be many times when you will want to sell your own products and you will be doing the packaging and shipping yourself. For instance, if you find a great supply of compact discs selling for under the wholesale price, you will want to buy them and sell them yourself using your Mail Order business. Once you finish reading this book you will know how to find merchandise selling for under the wholesale price and how to mark it up so you can make up to a 500% profit margin.

For now we need to learn the basic ingredient of setting up the fulfillment aspect of your Mail Order operation so you can start making money as soon as possible. There are two steps in shipping out an order. The first one consists of determining if the order has been fully paid for and what the order consists of. After you have done this by looking at your records you will know what to include in the shipment. The next step in the assembling of the order is the packaging. The packaging is very important because it will be the first impression the customer has about your operation. A professionally wrapped package will tell the customer that you have taken the time and effort to unsure that his order arrived in one piece. The inside of the box should be layered with a few layers of tissue wrap. The last thing you want is for the merchandise to become damaged while in transit. Enclose the actual item in a small watertight plastic bag in case the box comes into contact with water. The customer will not mind a wet box as long as his merchandise is safe and sound. You can use bubble wrap to further insulate the package. The box that you enclose the merchandise in should be double layered, or one box inside the other. Many people insist on using UPS for their deliveries. UPS will pick up the package from your house and deliver to the doorstep of your customer. The United Parcel Service has its own requirements that a package must meet before they will ship it. On the other hand the postal service is more lenient and also provides a great value because of their lower prices. Besides the price difference the big advantage of using UPS is that you can set up an account with them and have them pick up packages from your house on a daily basis. This way you will not have to run to the post office every time you want to mail out an order. Imagine running to the post office every day and waiting for an hour on line before you can hand your packages to the window teller. And even then you will still have to wait for the packages to be weighted so you can be charged. If you use UPS you might have to pay a little more but it is worth it for the convenience that they provide. There are also other shippers such as Fed Ex that are great for smaller packages that need to be mailed out express. I have used all three-delivery services and can attest that they all do a great job and each offer unique advantages.

You can start out by splitting up your shipping between UPS and the US Postal Service. You might enjoy using one more for certain packages while some of your customers might want the other shipper. An important detail to remember is that UPS does not deliver to post office boxes so you will have to use the post office in those situations. One more thing that I like about UPS is that they require the person accepting the package to sign for it. This way you have proof that they got the package. If you use the postal service you can pay a small fee to request that the person should sign for the package, even if he or she has a post office box. As far as buying the supplies you will need to do the packaging you can either buy them at the post office or at any shipping outlet. In my area there is a chain of stores that sells packaging materials. They also act as UPS pick up centers so you can mail your packages through them. They will charge you a small fee on top of what UPS charges them to ship the product. They provide convenience and are useful when you cannot wait at home for UPS to pick up your packages. People who conduct Mail Order businesses in addition to a full time job cannot be at home when UPS does their pick ups. They usually drop off their packages at night to one of the shipping stores and let the store worry about mailing out their product. For an extra small charge the store can even pack your merchandise. You just need to leave them with the mailing labels and be very clear which items goes in which box. I used this method a few times and it was a great time save for those really busy days. I dropped off the merchandise in milk containers. Each milk container had a sheet of paper on top of it indicating my return address and the mailing address. The store then would pack everything up and affix shipping labels that they wrote up. I would then stop off at the end of the day and pay for the packaging and mailing services after carefully looking at the recite. I was not concerned about their honesty; I was more concerned that there should be no clerical mistakes in writing down the mailing addresses or computing what I owed them. If you develop a strong relationship with the shipping outlet you can even arrange to drop off merchandise all week long and pay your bill at the end of the week. This way you have time to let your money sit in the bank and collect interest while the packing and shipping have already been taken care of. You are in business to make money and any extra money that you can make will help you move forward towards achieving your goals.

CHAPTER 7

Develop A Business Plan
For Your Mail Order Business

Your business plan will serve as the blue print to build your business. The business plan will have information that will keep you focused on your business. You should use this book to develop a business plan that you can use to run your business. The purpose of the business plan is to map out the actions that you will be taking to start and expand your business into a multi million-dollar operation. The best time to write the business plan is when you are excited and full of ideas. You should begin by writing down the basic idea behind your Mail Order business. Write the way you think. You are not writing the business plan to impress anyone so write it the way that you will feel the most comfortable when using it. You can add on ideas to the business plan as you think of them and cross out ideas that you no longer like. The business plan is a document that will fluctuate with time and with the development of your venture. Even though the plan might look entirely different a year after you have started the business it is still intrinsic that you have one. Because you will be suing the business plan to determine what your next step should be. You will be using it as an instructional manual that you devised to grow your company. It is very common for someone to come up with a great strategy to make money and then forget about it a few weeks later. To avoid this problem and establish yourself as a successful Mail Order entrepreneur you will write down all of your strategies in your business plan. This way when you forget an idea you will only have to look at the plan to remind yourself. The importance of the business plan increases when your business expands and you start pursuing different channels of sales. I can promise you that things will seem more complicated when you try to sell five different lines of products in five different newspapers, three catalogs, and 10 classified ads. But if you have a business plan you will always know what to do next and what the focus of your business is. I have provided the outline of a sample business plan that you are welcome to use. Feel free to copy it exactly or modify it as your business grows. Since the purpose of this plan will be to guide your business the plan will consist of the main components that a successful Mail Order business must have.

The business plan will consist of a general description of the aims of your venture; this section is referred to as the executive summary, a marketing plan, a market summary, management section, and a financial section. You will be surprised at how much easier it will be to start and conduct your business once you have written out a business plan so I highly suggest that you spend the time writing one up.

The executive summary will contain all the basic information about your Mail Order business. This is the section in which you write what the purpose of your business will be. You want to write down what type of products you will be dealing with and who your market will be. Imagine that you are reading about a successful business a year after it was launched. The reporter writing the article needs to write a short summary making it perfectly clear what the business is and what it does. The reporter needs to convey in a few paragraphs the essence of the business. You need to play the part of the reporter when writing your business plan. Put yourself in the shoes of the reporter and picture the thousands of people who will read your summary. If they can understand the basic premise behind your business you will be on the right track. The better of a job you do explaining your business the easier it will be for you to stay focused. You will always be able to look back at your executive summary and remember exactly what the purpose and goals of your business are. If you plan on selling cooking recipes through classified ads you need to right that down in your summary. This way even if you get sidetracked for a few weeks and forget exactly what product you initially wanted to sell you can look at your executive summary for the answer.

A sample executive summary could be written this way:

Lowy Enterprises is a Mail Order business selling movies through the mail. The business will buy movies at below wholesale prices and resell them at 50% below retail to the general public. The target customer base for Lowy Enterprises is comprised of 18 to 25 year olds with disposable income who enjoy actively purchasing movies. The majority of the advertising will be done through small display ads in entertainment magazines. I plan on developing a catalog to send out to my customers to encourage follow up orders. I will obtain my merchandise from movie wholesalers with overstock and video stores going out of business. My goal is to develop a customer base of 5,000 customers within 12 months and to sell a minimum of 2000 movies a month while continuing to expand my customer base.

The actual executive summary you use should be more detailed and should be at least two pages long. I know that having to write two pages requires effort and time but it will be worth it when you realize how much of a difference it will make in your business. The executive summary is the section where you can write down all of your ideas. You can have a chapter devoted towards ideas that you will consider doing as your business grows. You might brainstorm and come up with ideas for selling auto parts, farm supplies, and painting supplies in your Mail Order Business. You might not be able to sell those three lines of products in the same catalog because of the typical customers who will buy each product. But you still want to include all three products in your business plan for future reference. You will still focus your business plan on only one of the three product lines, but by having them all down on paper you can always expand into them later on when your business is larger. Some Mail Order enthusiasts take too much upon themselves when they first start out. Avoid this situation by starting with only one product line that you are familiar with. Later on you can hire an assistant to help you work with a second line of merchandise while you focus on your original product line. You might not need to hire an assistant if you are organized enough to avoid get swamped with trying to keep up with all your orders. Initially you should still focus on only one product line so you can fully devote yourself to marketing it to the fullest. Believe me when I tell you that you can make a great deal of money selling one product to 10,000 customers. It might sound better to have five different products than only one but the bottom line is not how many products you have but how much you are selling. When you devote yourself to one product line you can spend all of your time for cheap methods to advertise it and sell the product. Instead of having to look for appropriate advertising channels for all of your product lines you only need to find one. Once you determine the best place for your one line of products you can immerse yourself in marketing it.

The next part of the business plan is the marketing section. Many large businesses have marketing plans that are longer than the rest of the business plan combined. The marketing plan for a Mail Order business is its oxygen tank. Just like a body needs a constant flow of oxygen, a Mail Order business needs a constant flow of marketing. The more marketing a business does the more customers it will be able to attract. A Mail Order business attracts a storefront that people can pass by and notice. The only storefront a Mail Order operation has is its advertisements. Without advertisements the public will never discover the company no matter how good its products or services are. So you should sit down and think out a good marketing plan for your business. You can attract a million customers to your business if you encourage them to become customers. Your ability to encourage them to become loyal customers will be based on your ability to come up with a solid publicity-generating plan. I will show you how you can implement a great marketing plan that produces results for little or no money. The plan is based on a few principles that I have learned in business and I will be more than glad to pass them on to you.

The marketing section is where you write down every idea you have for promoting your product or service. You should list every idea you and your family can come up with. If you are running the business by yourself, like many Mail Order entrepreneurs do, you can generate ideas by reading marketing books and real accounts of Mail Order companies. I recently read a book that described how a housewife built a hundred million dollar Mail Order business from her kitchen. She advertised women's fashion accessories that she designed from home. She placed a few ads in different women's magazines and soon received a few thousand orders. She repeated her advertisements this time offering an expanded selection of accessories she was making and proceeded to make more money than her husband was in his full time job. Her company now has sales in the hundreds of millions of dollars every year.

Or what about the college student who wrote a book on how to obtain scholarships? He sold 25,000 copies his first year alone from his house. I am estimating that if he made $4 a copy (which is a very conservative number) he would have made a $100,000 profit. And since there is nothing stopping him from selling the book year after year he could be looking at a steady income of $100,000 for a very long time.

How did he do it? He approached many bookstores and offered to have signings for his book in their stores. He brought the books and sold them to all the people who came to listen to him. He also listed his book through the online booksellers and increased his sales beyond his expectations. His total cost of advertising was minimal since he let the bookstores advertise that he would be appearing at their stores. He came up with an innovative idea that has generated him at least $100,000 in profits by my estimates.

This is the time for you to come up with your own innovative ideas for promoting your business so you too can make over $100,000 a year. I know that you want to jump right into the business and start right away, but the extra patience that you demonstrate now will help you increase your level of income in the near future.

Here is an example of a marketing section using the continuing example of Lowy Enterprises.

Lowy Enterprises plans on marketing its selection of videos using innovative concepts that will reach the consumer directly. One method will be to place classified advertisements in movie magazines for a catalog. I will request $2 per catalog so I can cover the cost of the classified ad, the cost of printing and mailing the catalog, and keep a.50 profit on each catalog request. I also plan on attracting customers by making up small catalogs and drop- ping them off at local colleges in my area. If I drop off 100 catalogs a week, after three months I will have placed 1200 catalogs in circulation. Even if I only gain 200 new customers it will be worth it since I can make up to $9 on each video I sell. Another market- ing strategy for my business is paying my local newspaper to in- sert a one-page movie list in the morning newspaper. This way I can reach 100,000 people without having to spend any money for printing ad mailing the catalogs. People will be able to order di- rectly from the catalog and place orders the same day they receive the newspaper. I also plan on looking for inexpensive display ads in regional publications that cater towards college students and recent graduates. I have included a list of possible publications I plan on using . . .

Your marketing plan should contain all the advertising and marketing methods that you can think of. You can later erase or add ideas as you think of them. The value of having a marketing section is that you will be able to keep a compendium of all of your promotion ideas. From time to time you will read articles in magazines that will give you inspiring ideas on how to market your Mail Order business. You might even read an article in a newspaper on how a company managed to reach its target customer base. After reading the article you will want to sit down and see how you can apply their strategy to your own pursuit of increasing your sales. The marketing section is where you will include the new information that you have come across.

The next section of your business plan is the market summary. In the market summary you are researching the market that you will be operating in. You want to research your potential market so you can analyze their wants and needs. You want to determine what products they are in the market for and products they currently buy. If I wanted to research the market for children's books I would contact a few children's magazines and ask them for their media kits. The media kits would contain information on the number of readers they have, that number is an indication on how big the market it is. The media kit would also tell me the level of income the average readers have and what they spend their money on. I can then see which products parents buy and how much money they spend on each product category. I can even be more direct and call the advertising magazine and ask them what the best product to advertise though their magazines would be. They will be candid and tell you which advertisers advertise the most. You can use that information to determine which products parents are most apt to buy for their children through the mail. You will know if children's books will sell well, or if you should sell another product that will result in greater profits.

The market summary will have as many facts and statistics you can gather on the market you are entering. If you want to sell booklets by mail you would want to comb the classified ads and see if there are others doing the same thing as you. If there many classified ads selling booklets then you know that there is a market in Mail Order for small information booklets. If there were no market for the booklets then there would not be people repeatedly placing classified ads selling information. Keep in mind that many of the ads are one-time ads and therefore you cannot draw any conclusions from them. The classified ads you want to look for are the ones that are placed more than once, since no one would place an ad again unless it was bringing in sales. The market summary is where you do all of the research that will determine the size and scope of the market. There is a market for every product as long as you are selling your product to the right market. Your research will point you in the right direction to ensure that you are selling to the right market.

Conducting research will also ensure that you price the product correctly. Just because people are selling millions of books a year does not mean that you can a book at any price you want. On the other hand, every segment of the book market will tolerate different prices. A lawyer will feel comfortable paying $35 for a book of the latest changes in his profession. But a high school student would not consider paying more than $8 for a popular novel. Publisher research their markets and determine what the most people will pay for their books and they price accordingly. Your market research will help you determine what you can price your merchandise for. You can easily find out the prices you should be charging by looking at the prices catalogs, stores, and Mail Order dealers charge.

Here is the market summary that I would write for the example business:

There are currently 20 million people in this country between the ages of 18 and 25. Out of that 20 million people an estimated 10 million buy movies on a weekly basis so my market consists of 10,000,000 people across the country. Most 18-25 year olds will only pay at most $10 for a movie so I need to price it below that to encourage them to buy from me. After doing my research I have found that I can purchase overstock and excess movies from various sources for an average of $2 a movie. I can sell the movies for $8 each and make money while offering my customers a 20% discount off the regular prices. I have also found that video stores purchase movies for $3 each so I plan on mailing them catalogs once a month with my selections. My research indicates that if I can capture.001 of the market I will have 100,000 customers. If I sell each customer one video at $8 each my gross revenues will be $800,000 giving me a profit of $600,000. Since my research indicates that the average person in this age group will purchase three movies in a year I will have the opportunity to sell 300,000 videos and net $1.8 million.

Statistics have shown that most videos are bought from catalogs so I plan on advertising the catalogs in entertainment magazines. I have saved all of my research in a file which I can look at to re examine my information as needed.

This example demonstrates the statistics and facts that you will be looking for so you can put your business on the right track and grow it into a million dollar operation. You might come across research that will help you discover a new opportunity you might have missed before. Many people discover a business opportunity inadvertently while researching another business. I have been actively investing in penny stocks for a few years and decided to write a book on the topic. I made this decision when I discovered that there was no detailed source of information on how to make investing and trading penny stocks. My book, The Guide For Penny Stock Investing, is doing very well, although you and I know that the only reason I though of writing it was because I could not find any information on the topic. You might discover a business opportunity while you are researching your Mail Order operation that can turn you into as millionaire. The next section that we will discuss is the management section of your business plan.

The management section details what skills will be needed to run the business and who will be supplying those skills. If you are not an accountant you will want to make a note in this section that you should look for one to help you when it comes to file your taxes. If your business will need someone to write advertisements you need to decide if you will make it your responsibility to learn how to write the ads or will you delegate the task to someone else. What ever your decisions are you need to make it very clear to yourself what skills and knowledge you will need for your business and how you will be ensuring that those requirements are fulfilled.

This section should supply you with a management plan for your Mail Order business as it grows in size. Decide what you will do when your sales double in size. Will you need additional staff?

What about when you are shipping 1000 orders a week? You need to come up with a plan of action for those situations in which the Mail Order business experiences a very strong demand. You need to have a contingency plan for in case you receive an unexpected amount of orders. Make sure you are ready if you place an ad in a million plus circulation magazine. If people love your ad and product you just might receive a tremendous amount of orders. You should have handy the phone numbers of a few college placement offices so you can call them up if you need a few extra workers for a really busy period. College students have flexible schedules and would love to help and make some extra money on the side.

The financial section of your plan is the section that will show you in black and white if you have a viable business. This section should be used to determine if your business could yield the profits you are looking for. You will obtain this answer by compiling all of your expected expenses and then subtracting your expenses from your projected sales. Your expenses consist of advertising, printing, renting a mailbox if you need one, and the cost of the product. Your projected sales should be conservative since you want to prepare for the situation in which you receive a minimal amount of orders. If you receive a larger than expected number of orders then you will be in luck since you have prepared well.

Although we will include the cost of advertising and the cost of the product, I will show you how you can eliminate both of these costs. But if you plan on producing your own product and would like the highest degree of freedom when advertising, you will then want to spend money both on the product and on the marketing. I can show you how you can profit tremendously from using some of my favorite methods that eliminate most Mail Order costs. At the same time I can guide you to increasing the size of your business by spending a small amount of money on products and marketing. Once you finish reading the book you will have a clear idea of which direction you will want to proceed in.

The financial section should start out with a paragraph listing every conceivable expense you might have. You can later cross out expenses if you find a way to either eliminate or reduce them. You can put down a ballpark figure for every expense. If you plan on spending $100 a month to advertise write down that figure next to your advertising expense. If you expect the cost of printing 1000 catalogs to be under $200 write down $200 as your expense to be on the safe side. Once you are done with your expenses I want you to write down your expected sales. To play it safe you should expect only 5% of your prospects to respond to your offer. This means that if you mail out 1000 catalogs only 50 people will initially respond and buy products. Five percent is a very low number and you might generate a much larger response rate but since we want to be conservative in our estimates we would rather err on the safe side. Even with only 50 orders per 1000 catalogs you can still make a great deal of money if your profit is $20 per order. And instead of only mailing out 1000 catalogs you will soon be mailing out 10,000 catalogs a month as your business grows.

If you are advertising in a magazine you should use a response rate of only 1%. Once again, I do believe that your response rate can be many times this number. But even using a response rate of only 1% you can still make a great deal of money. For example, if the magazine you are advertising in has a circulation of 500,000 readers, a one percent response rate would mean 5,000 buyers. Even if your profit per item was only $2 you will still have earned a $10,000 profit.

Here is a sample of a financial statement using Lowy Enterprises.

Sales:

5% of Catalogs= 2500 orders. Minimum order is one video at $8= $20,000

Charge Customers $2 for each Catalog request= $100,000

Classified advertisement for catalog with a total circulation of 1,000,000 gives me a response rate of 50,000 based on 1,000,000 x.01=50,000

Total revenues $20,000 for videos plus $100,000 for catalog request= $120,000

Expenses:

Mailbox rental= $72 for the year

Advertising= $300 per month

Catalogs= (50,000) $5,000 Entire supply for the year based on.10 per ten page catalog.

Mailing Expense=.19 per catalog is $9500

Cost of video= $2 x 2500 units is $5,000

Total expenses= $5,000 + $5,000 + $300 + $72= $10,732

The total revenues in this example total $120,000 and the expenses total $20,232. Therefore the net profits for this Mail Order business is $99,268.

The profits of this mail order business would triple if the classified advertisement brought in a response rate of 3% instead of a 1% rate. Imagine what would happen if the response rate was %6? The total profits would close in at $600,000!

The financial statement will enable you to set up a budget for your business. You will know how much money you will need to have upfront before starting your business. The reason that I love Mail Order is because you do not need to have allotted a large amount of money to start. If you look at the above example, you will see that the only expense you need to pay upfront is the mailbox and advertising expense. You only have to pay for the catalogs once you receive orders for them. And since you are receiving $2 per catalog you can use that money to print and mail the catalogs. Your cost for printing and mailing the catalogs (.29) comes out of the $2 you receive. The only cost you need to pay before you receive any orders is the mailbox rent and the cost of advertising. You can eliminate the cost of the mailbox if you use your home address for the address of your business. At that point your only upfront expense would be $300 for the cost of the ad. You can start out with a smaller circulation magazine that charges less for its classified ads. One word of advice, if you find that you will need $200 to start your business you should budget $400 for your business. By budgeting twice what you will need you are protecting yourself against any unexpected costs. The rate of advertising might increase before you get a chance to renew your ad so you want to have the extra money to still be able to purchase the ad. Or the publisher might offer you a better rate if you are willing to buy two ads instead of one. By having the extra money you can take advantage of profitable opportunities that you will come across.

CHAPTER 8

Get Good Accounting Advice

A good accountant will verify your numbers and ensure that your financials balance out. You should obtain the advice of a good accountant to guide you when you are making financial decisions. A seasoned accountant will have experience built up from working for other clients. He will be able to supply you with ideas on how to minimize your costs and keep track of your expenses. His services will pay off when he shows you how to save money and conduct your business in a more organized fashion. When tax season comes he will be able to use his knowledge to reduce your tax liability by taking advantage of every deduction that you are entitled of.

The same way that doctors specialize in particular segments, accountants also specialize. An accountant will develop a client list based on the field that he works on. So while one client might have a client base consisting of retail storeowners, another accountant will primarily deal with medical practices. You want to make sure that your accountant works with Mail Order clients. Chances are that the accountant will have other clients besides his Mail Order clients. You want to ensure that the Mail Order client you use has experience in the Mail Order field since you will be relying on his advice to increase the profitability of his business. There are many unique accounting issues that relate to the operation of a Mail Order operation that a less experienced accountant might be ignorant of. Make sure to find and use the services of an experienced accountant.

You can locate an accountant by opening your phone book

and calling a few of the accountants listed. Interview them by asking them how long they have been working for, what type of clients they work with, and if they have done work for a Mail Order business.

CHAPTER 9

Connect With An Experienced Lawyer.

You might decide to protect your business by incorporating. If you decide to incorporate make sure that you have an experienced lawyer doing the paperwork for you. You do not want to be sued and then find out that since you never properly incorporated you are now personally liable. A good lawyer can also give you advice on the proper wording for an advertisement, the content of a catalog, agreements between you and a supplier and many other items that can arise as you conduct your business. A good lawyer will cost money but can easily keep your business on the right track. You can run into legal issues because you omitted a few words form your ad, so make sure that you have an attorney that you trust look over your ad copy. I would not recommend anyone even acting on the information from this book before they obtain legal advice. I do not want to overtly stress the importance of a lawyer but is very important to always confer with an attorney before engaging in any business venture.

You can find a good lawyer by asking your family and friends if they know of any good lawyer who has done work for them. You should not have to ask more than five people before you are given the phone number of a good attorney. Once you do call the attorney ask him for an initial consultation in which you can discuss if you are appropriate for each other. I am sure that if the lawyer feels that he lacks knowledge to help you he will refer you to an experienced business lawyer.

CHAPTER 10

Convey Trust

The mail Order operator has to over come the reluctance of a customer to buy a product they have never seen before. The customer might be interested in ordering the product but because they have never seen it or felt it in their own hands they will be reluctant to place an order. You can overcome this reluctance by ensuring that if they do not like the product they will not be stuck with it. Offering a guarantee on all products that you sell encourages the prospective buyer to place an order. The prospective buyer will place an order knowing that in the event that they are not happy with the product they can return it for a full refund. The refund they will receive is only for the cost of the product and not for the shipping and handling charge. Once they see that you offer a guarantee they place an order with confidence knowing that in the even that they are not satisfied they will receive a prompt refund.

Offering a guarantee on your products also tells prospective buyers that you firmly believe that they will be happy. If you did not believe that they would be happy you would not offer a very generous return policy. Think about it, if someone is selling a product that he is sure no one will ever return, he can afford to offer a one-year guarantee. If you read an advertisement for a product offering a one-year guarantee you would know that the seller expects you to be so happy that in the following 12 months you will never even think about returning it. You will then order from this ad knowing that in the event that you are not happy you can always send it back. The same approach works if you are the one doing the selling. If your catalog offers a 12-month return policy you will receive many more orders since people will know that they can always get their money back if they are not satisfied. At this point you must be wondering if I am concerned with having a tremendous amount of returns a few months down the line. The reasoning being that once someone has used a product once, or for a few months, they will simply send it back and ask for a refund. But the reality is that people do not like to go through the trouble of sending something back. And to ensure that people do not take advantage of your offer you can ask for a detailed explanation of why they are returning the product. At this point, usually only people who are returning the product for legitimate reasons will proceed to send it back to you.

The type of product that you sell should determine the guarantee that you offer. You do not wan to offer an unconditional return policy on a product that the customer can easily break. You do not want the customer to use the product for a few months and then return it if he or she damages it. On the other hand, if you do offer a guarantee that it will not break within a certain amount of time you will have more orders. Customers will order the product knowing that there is a quality assurance. You can also eliminate many fraudulent returns by requiring the customer to pay the mailing costs for returning any product. For the most part, people are honest and will not take advantage of you. But by protecting yourself you will save yourself from many hours of aggravation.

Customers are just as concerned that they are dealing with an honest company when ordering products so you will need to build their trust. By promising them a guarantee and following it you will win their trust. Even if a customer returns a product he might be interested in ordering from you. It is worth accepting a return if by doing so the customer will enjoy doing business with you and place 20 more orders in his lifetime. Keep your word and you will develop a lifetime base of customers.

CHAPTER 11

Your Best Endorsement

The highest endorsement a business can receive is the one given to it by customers. Customers are very frank when it comes to talking about how they feel about a business. If they are upset they will let you know in very clear terms. When customers are happy they sometimes drop you a note or call you to let you know that they appreciate your service. The difference is that when people are upset about an event they make it their business to let people know, but when they are happy they usually go on their way without giving feedback to the company. You should try to always solicit positive feedback from your customers. The reason is that you can show the positive feedback to prospective customers to encourage them to buy from you. If they like what other customers have said they will be inclined to placing an order with you.

Testimonials are one of the most effective tools a Mail Order entrepreneur can use to make money. The testimonials are proof that people like his or her products. And customers will realize that if many other people liked the products of the Mail Order firm they will probably also enjoy them. You should use testimonials in every opportunity when you are trying to convince someone to place an order. If you have display ad you can include a one-line sentence from your happiest customer. If you have a catalog you should place one testimonial on the top pf each page. This way customers are continually reminded about how much people liked their products.

If you do decide to use testimonials you need to keep the original feedback from the customer on file. This insures that testimonials are not fabricated. If you do not have any testimonials you can either ask your customers to write to you with their comments, or you can ask people to sample your product and give you an honest opinion on how they feel about it.

CHAPTER 12

Service Is Your Business

As a Mail Order business the degree of service that you offer will help you capture a large degree of the market. Many Mail Order firms fall lax in the service they give because they do not see the customer in front of them. They allow the customer to become just another order instead of remembering that the customer is a person with needs and desires that need to be met. You should differentiate yourself from your competition by always treating your customers as individuals. By treating them like individuals you will develop a connection with them that can last years. Once you have developed a two-way connection with your customers they will be inclined towards placing more orders with you. They place more orders with you because they trust you and feel that you are attentive to their needs as a person.

You should establish this connection with them by providing a very high degree of service. When you provide a high degree of service they will be impressed and realize that you care about them. Everyone wants to do business with someone who personally cares about his or her personal welfare. You can demonstrate that you care about your customers' personal welfare by going out of your way to ensure that they are happy with their order. The first step in doing this is to send them a thank you note with every order and sending them a follow up letter a few weeks after they have received the order. Most people do not expect to hear from you after they have received your order and will be very impressed that if you have taken out the time to follow up with them. In your follow up letter you should first thank them for giving you their business and then ask them if they are satisfied with the product or service they have received. You can enclose a stamped post card so they realize how much you want to hear from them.

This way if a customer is not happy with your product you still have a chance to talk to him. If you do not contact him he will simply forget about your company and never place another order. But if the customer writes back that he is not happy you can find out why and try to make up for the shortcoming. You can offer a discount on his next order, free shipping, or a free bonus. This way you can take a negative experience and turn it into a positive one. Instead of loosing the customer you can end up selling more to him and make even more money than if he had only bought once from you.

There are many customers who planned on only ordering once from you. They were only interested in the product that you were offering at the time. You can even turn them into repeat customers if you follow up and contact them. You can customers to tell you what type of products they are interested in. You can then take this information and use it to sell the right products to your customers. If you know that the one time customer likes music, you can put together a small catalog of tapes and compact discs and mail it to him. He will then have an opportunity to place another order since this time he is being offered products that he is always interested in. This small service technique can turn any one-time customer into a lifetime customer.

The key to providing service is to always be courteous and optimistic in all of your communication with the customer. Instead of falling into arguments with the customer let the customer always be right. This way you might have to lose on one sale but you will have gained a customer for life.

CHAPTER 13

Mail Order Success Stories

The Mail Order field is full of stories of entrepreneurs who have succeeded beyond their expectations. The ability of an individual to start a business for less than $500 is very appealing to people who do not want to risk a great deal of money when starting a business. The fact that you can make an enormous amount of money in the Mail Order business with a very small investment is what makes this business so attractive.

You can start this business from your home and eliminate the need to rent a store or an office. While most businesses require you to spend thousands of dollars a month on rent, your rent expenses are zero. You do not have to pay a landlord rent, or give him a two-month security deposit, or pay insurance for your store. All of your rent expenses can be eliminated. Another expense that puts a strong dent in many solid businesses is the salary of employees. As a Mail Order operator you do not have any employees to pay so your salary expenses are zero. Most of your out of pocket expenses are so trivial that even the most spend thrift individual can start a Mail Order business.

You do not have to worry about seasonal drops in business. Your overhead is zero because you are running it from home so you are not under pressure to produce orders every week. You can even make enough money working 6 months and take a break the rest of the year. You have no obligation to keep your business open all year round.

The biggest challenge that people who want to go into business face is the risk. The risk that they are afraid of the most is if their business goes belly up they will be left without a source of income. The Mail Order business caters to those people who do not want to be left without their regular source of paychecks. This is because you can run a Mail Order business part time while holding a full time job. You can do this by limiting the hours you spend on your business to when you come home form work. What if you are too tired to put in an hour after work every day? You can process and ship your orders on the weekends. This will mean giving up most of your free time on the weekends, but it can translate into a million dollar business.

Once your Mail Order business starts producing the results you are aiming for you can leave your full time job. This way you already know how much money your Mail Order business is bringing in and can determine if the income is adequate to sustain the lifestyle you envision. The Mail Order business is perfect for those who are between jobs and have a small cushion of savings to live on until the orders start rolling in.

Here are some examples of Mail Order entrepreneurs who have done very well with their business. One entrepreneur sells millions of dollars of information booklets from his home office. The booklets cost him about .25 each to print and he sells them for as much as $25 each. He has other Mail Order dealers who sell his booklets for him. This way he can reach even more customers through the marketing efforts of the other Mail Order dealers.

A housewife who started her business by selling clothing accessories from her kitchen table grew it into a giant catalog company. Today her business has sales in the hundreds of millions.

Another Mail Order company sells hard cover books across the country to busy consumers who do not have the time to shop in the stores.

A recent upstart sells high quality clothing that is not available in stores. Consumers have come to recognize the high level of quality clothing that this fashionable Mail Order catalog sells.

A monthly catalog sells discounted electronics that are bought from manufacturers overstocks and closeout sales. This catalog sells its merchandise at up to 90% off retail.

A sleek catalog sells hundreds of thousands of dollars of skiing equipment to ardent skiers.

Another colorful and thick catalog has been selling car radios and music accessories to drivers for over 25 years.

There is an entrepreneur who has sold millions of dollars of magazine subscriptions without having to ever leave his office.

There was an individual who sells $10,000 a month worth of perfumes from his basement.

One of the largest comic book dealers sells entirely by mail. His sales are larger than any comic book store and his entire business consists of a catalog.

You can be the next Mail Order success story if you put your heart into it and use the information in this book to build your business.

CHAPTER 14

Internet Riches

The Internet can help your Mail Order business grow exponentially. The Internet is a communication medium that brings together millions of people on a daily basis. There are millions of people who log on to the Internet to do their shopping, research a project, look for business information, and look for a job. People use the Internet because of the convenience that it offers and the ease of access to countless information. Before the advent of the Internet if someone wanted to locate a product she would first have to comb through the phone book calling stores until she found the product. If the stores did not have the product she would then have to try to find a catalog that featured the product. Even if she found a catalog with the right product now she would have to see if the price is fair. Even after ordering the product the customer would have to wait another few weeks until she received it. The entire process from beginning to end could take over a month until the customer has the product in her hands. But now with the advent of the Internet the same customer can simply log on and do a search for the same product. Within a few seconds the customer will be presented with a list of thousands of web sites offering the product.

The reason that the Internet is such an effective tool for finding what ever you are looking for is because it consists of web sites set up all across the country by millions of people. The cost of setting up a web site is often free so many businesses quickly set up a site to sell their merchandise. You can easily find all of their web sites since each site has key words that the search engine reads when looking for the information that you have requested.

For instance, if you are looking for a site with the phrase "free advertising", the search engine will compile a list of all the sites using the key words free and advertising in their descriptions. You can also conduct a search for the exact phrase so the list of sites will consist entirely of web sites offering free advertising.

There are an estimated 50 million people using the Internet every month with that number expected to triple within 2 years. That means that every month you have a market of 50,000,000 potential customers every month. The best part is that these customers are actively looking for products and information. If you can supply the products and services they are looking for you stand to reap the profits from having millions of customers. While everyone is on the Internet for different reasons there are some characteristics that are constant for all of them. They are all looking for the opportunity to improve their quality of life. Think about it, what person doesn't want to be richer, better looking, smarter, healthier, or better off?

Everyone is looking to improve his or her lives in some fashion. Human nature dictates that we will always be involved in the pursuit of a higher lifestyle. This desire is what leads to technological innovations and dynamic inventions. If people were satisfied with whatever state their lives were in they would be not be looking to make more money, or to compete. But what makes people so special is their desire to continuously improve themselves and the state of the world.

You can tap into this desire by catering your business to sell products that enable people to improve their lives. Products such as vitamins, books, exercise equipment, business opportunities, job information, training, and hygiene products, enable people to improve their lifestyles. These products directly fulfill the needs of people looking to maker things better for themselves and for their families. It is up to you to decide which product category you will be selling. If you are able to match a product to a need that millions of people experience you will have a good chance of selling millions of your products.

The other approach that works great on the Internet is selling to a niche. A niche is a small segment of the market that is looking for a specific product or service. A market for clothing could consist of a small niche for religious clothing. While the over all market is not interested in religious clothing there will always be a small amount of people looking for religious clothing. Often, because of the size of the niche the larger Mail Order companies over look it. They do not feel that it is cost effective to set up their businesses to sell a product for which there is a relatively small number of customers. But with the advent of the Internet not only does it become cost effective to sell to a niche but you can also make a great deal of money doing so. You can make a great deal of money selling to a small niche because while the number of people may be small you will often face no competition. You could be the only Mail Order company selling cowhide wallets to farmers located in Wisconsin. Even though there might only be 100 farmers who are looking for cowhide wallets you will be the only one who selling them.

The Internet also enables you to realize the potential of selling to a niche that is often overlooked. There might only be 1000 farmers in Wisconsin looking for your product. But once you advertise on the Internet your product will be exposed to millions of users. Framers from across the country will see your product and have the opportunity to place an order. Even though there might only be 20 people in each city looking for your product the orders will add up once you multiply that number by the number of cities. Every neighborhood has people with unique interested that are not served by their local stores or Mail Order catalogs. If you sell the product they are looking for then you will have all those people who cannot find their desired product as customers. Even if only one out of every 300 people are interested in the home-made t-shirts you have made you will still have a tremendous amount of interest. There are 250,000,000 people in this country so even if you tap into small niche that only caters to one out every 1000 people you can still do very well. At a rate of 1 out of 2000 people the number of interested people across the country is 125,000. When you realize that even the smallest niche grows in size when looked at from a countrywide point of view you will realize how much money you can make. This is because even if only 50 people in every city are interested in your product there are hundreds of cities across the country. So the number of interested people increased when you count every interested person in every city.

The beauty of the Internet is that it is open to everyone. Anyone who has access to a computer can easily access the Internet and start shopping. Today, most web sites allow customers to place their orders directly on the site. This allows the customer to place an order without having to go through the trouble of trying to get in touch with the company. The customer can even place an order if he is shopping at 3 in the morning. Since everything is automated the customer can complete the entire order without having to speak to the company. The Internet is perfect for busy people who work the entire day and never seem to have the time to do their shopping. You can even order your groceries online. There are thousands of reasons why people shop on the Internet ranging from cheap prices to product selection to being able to find niche products. It is up to you to make sure that your products are available on the Internet so you can capture this market.

The advantage of running your Mail Order business on the Internet is vast. You can reach more people using the Internet than you can with any other medium including the television. There are over 50 million people using the Internet every month. On a typical night there are millions of Americans checking their email, looking up information, or shopping in their favorite web site. The reason that the Internet is so effective is because people can play an active role. The television only allows the viewer to watch the programming. The Internet allows the surfer to decide what he or she wants to see.

Another difference between the television and the Internet is the style of advertising. Commercials on TV last only 30 seconds and are instantly replaced by the next commercial. Even if someone likes a product featured on a commercial he only has 30 seconds to find a pen and paper and write the phone number on the screen down. Advertisements on the web appear as part of the page you are viewing. The advertisement will be there until the person moves on to the next page. This means that a prospect will see your ad on the Internet for as long as he or she is reading the page. If the prospect likes the ad they can take their time to find a pen and paper to write down the information from the ad. This style of advertising is very similar to the advertisements found in newspapers.

Although Internet and newspaper advertisements seem similar there is an immense advantage to advertising on the Internet over a newspaper. An ad in a newspaper is not interactive. The reader has only two choices when looking at an ad in the newspaper. He can either decide to place an order for the product or move on to the next page. His decision will be made based on the information provided on the ad. If the ad lacks enough information the reader might ignore the ad even if he was initially interested in the product. The Internet solves the problem of not providing enough information. The way that the Internet can ensure to always provide enough information is because it uses interactive technology. The reader of an Internet ad can click on the ad and be transported to the web site of the advertiser. This means that the advertiser can place thousands of ads that when clicked on bring the prospects directly to his web site. Once the prospects are at the web site they can be provided with more information. The ad might only be large enough to contain a three-line description of the item, but a web site can have an unlimited amount of pages.

Your web site can consist of your catalog along with a description of the products. This way the prospect will receive enough information to make his decision instead of ignoring the ad because of a lack of information. The value of the web site is that once the prospect is at your site you can offer him many more products than you could fit in the ad. A typical newspaper display ad is one square inch. At one square inch you could probably effectively promote one product. But with your own web site you can promote thousands of products. And once you turn your prospect into a repeat visitor you will have chance of making further repeat sales. A newspaper ad will only sell once while your web site can continuously sell.

You can turn a prospect into a long-term visitor by including useful information on the site. The information should closely pertain to your product line. You want your customers to consider your site an authority in your field. If you are selling electronics you should have a few columns explaining the difference between different products on the market and which ones give the best value. The more information you provide the more of a reason people will want to visit your site. The goal is to have people visiting your site even when they are not in the market to purchase merchandise. This way once they decide to make a purchase they will think of your web site.

Another effective tool to building up a following for your web site is to start a free newsletter. You can ask them to sign in when visiting your site so you can compile a list of visitors. You can then write a weekly newsletter and send it out over the Internet to all of your visitors. The cost of sending out an email is zero so you can send out thousands of newsletters for free. The newsletter will help keep your site in people's minds. People might come to your site just to subscribe to the newsletter. I know of one financial site that has over 20,000 people on its newsletter list. Every time they send out a newsletter they include an advertisement for a product. The cost of sending out the newsletter was free so the web site owner is not risking anything by sending it out. If 5% of the people receiving the newsletter buy the product he is selling he will have 1,000 orders. That is 1000 orders every week just for emailing out a newsletter.

You can develop your own newsletter or you can advertise on someone else newsletter. You can advertise for as low as $2 per

10,000 emails. That means that it will cost you 0.0002 per prospect. I dare you to try to find a cheaper place to advertise. Internet advertising is the cheapest medium because the costs of are so incredibly cheap for the publisher of the newsletter and the web site owner.

You can make even more money by creating your own newsletter and offering advertising spaces on it. You can write a one-page newsletter and have a second page with 10 advertisements. If you have 50,000 people on your list you can charge $10 per advertiser, or $100 for all ten ads. Multiply that number by 52 weeks and you will have made $5200 for hardly doing any work. The best part is that the entire $5200 is all profit. But what if you used your list of 50,000 email addresses and sent them 20 different newsletters? Instead of only making $5200 from one newsletter you are now making $104,000 from the advertisements in 20 newsletters!

It only gets better when you take the next step in increasing your revenue. You can make even more money by including your own ad in the newsletter. You can sell a $10 booklet on business opportunities on the Internet. People are always looking for an opportunity to make money and would appreciate a booklet teaching them how to make money with the Internet.

Since you own the newsletter you can place your ad on the first page so everyone notices your ad first. If you are able to get a 5% response rate from the 50,000 copies you send out you will have 2500 responses. At that rate you will get twenty-five hundred people who are interested in buying your book. That means that you will have sold 2500 books at $10 each. The ad will have grossed $25,000. Assuming that your cost per booklet is under a dollar each your total profit will be over $22,000. You will have just made over $22,000 from sending out a newsletter with your ad. If you send out the newsletter 52 times a year and are able to generate a 5% response rate each time you can generate over $240,000 in profits. And this number is on top of the revenue you will bring in from selling ads on your newsletter. You can see now why the Internet is such a productive money making tool. Even if you do not use a newsletter you can still make a great of money by taking your Mail Order business on the Internet.

You can generate millions of dollars from your web site by offering a vast array of products and attracting a large number of visitors to your site. You can attract visitors to your site by placing small inexpensive ads on other people's newsletters like we previously discussed. You can also place ads in other people's web sites directing them to your site. You will have to pay more to place an ad in a very frequently visited site. Some web sites charge over $30,000 for a full-page ad on their site. This cost is usually more than most starting Mail Order entrepreneurs can afford. But there is a very cost effective method for bringing in thousands of visitors to your site that can cost you virtually nothing.

This method works by pairing up with another web site that is also in need of visitors. You start out by contacting the owner of the web site and invite him to check out your site. Tell him that you are interested in exchanging ad space with him for the right to place an ad on his site. You will then both have a free ad on each other's site. You can find the contact information for the web site on its home page. Once you have placed an ad on his site your advertisement will be exposed to his visitors. If you can form this agreement with 10 different sites your ad will be exposed to all of the viewers of those 10 sites.

Make sure that the web sites cater to an audience that would be interested in the products that you are selling. If you are selling low fat food you want to advertise on sites catering to people trying to lose weight. If your web site is dedicated towards selling information on remodeling a house you will want to advertise on sites catering to homebuyers.

Another effective method of advertising your site is through an affiliate program. In an affiliate program you allow other sites to link to your site. When a buyer clicks on a link on their site and arrives at your site you give the originating site a commission on the purchases of the visitor. The site will advertise your services because they will want their visitors to go and make purchases at your site. To keep other web sites motivated to promote your site offer them a 10% commission on all purchases that a buyer makes who came from one of their sites. There are plenty of computer programs that allow you to set up affiliate programs. Once you have your affiliate program you can sing up hundreds of web sites that can bring you hundreds of thousands of visitors a month. Just imagine the money you can make if every visitor was to make a purchase.

The best part of having a web site is that you do not have to spend money printing and mailing out your catalogs. A majority of catalogs that are mailed out are not even looked at before they are disposed of. A web site only requires to be hosted and can be viewed by millions of people without having to mail them anything. The only cost you will face is paying a hosting company to host your web site. The hosting fee ranges from as low as $10 a month to as high as $40 depending on the number of pages you have and the size of the traffic you experience. You can have a web site hosted fro free if you agree to let the hosting company place ads on your site. This arrangement is appropriate if your Mail Order business is not based on selling ads on your site. Your business should be to sell products by mail, so it might be worth it to give up advertising rights on your sight in exchange for free hosting. Two companies that will host your site fro free are zoom.com and bigstep.com. You can go to their web sites and design your site straight from their web site. You can even upload pictures and content to make your site look even more professional. Once you have designed your site you need to register it with the search engines so people will be able to find your site when they search for the product that you offer.

Another great Internet tool that you can use to expand your Mail Order business is classified ads. There are thousands of web sites that offer free classified advertisements. They allow you to write up an ad and designate a classification for it. The ads usually run for about a month and you can place as many of them as you

would like. You can either try to sell directly from the free classified ads or you can supply an address or phone number so people
can request a catalog. Many classified ads are used to direct people
to web sites from which they can then make purchases.

The web sites that offer the free classified ads are hoping to
attract visitors to their site who will read and place ads. The same
way that many people pick up newspapers just to read the classified ads there are people who go to web sites just to read the classified ads. By allowing people to place free classified ads the web
site can generate more visitors who will also look at the rest of the
site once they are finished reading the ad section.

You can benefit from the exposure the free classified ads can
give your business. 100,000 people can see a free classified ad in
one web site alone in a month. If you place your free ad in 100
different sites you will have the potential to reach millions of people
for free. There are even services that will place your ad in hundreds
of sites for a small cost. You can write your ad once and pay them
$25 and they will place your ad in every free classified site on their
database. This technique alone can put your classified ad in the
face of millions of people who might never read the newspaper
that you have placed your other ads in.

I strongly recommend that people use all the available Internet
technology to maximize exposure of their business in conjunction
with print advertising. Print advertising should still be the backbone
of your Mail Order business. The reason that you need hard copy
advertising is because most Mail Order transactions are still
conducted in response to direct mail and catalogs. While an
increasing number of people are making their purchases from web
sites, a majority of people still buys their products from catalogs as
opposed to from web sites. The JC Penny catalog had $3.9 billion
worth of sales for the last 12 months. People are still buying using
catalogs and print advertising. In order to make it really big in
Mail Order you will need to combine print and online advertising.

CHAPTER 15

Meet Large Consumer Demand

The key to running a successful Mail Order business is to sell the highest amount of products at the highest profit possible that the market will allow. The more products that you sell the more money you will make. But in order to be able to sell allot of products you need to market your product to as many people as possible. Since we have determined that we will only expect a 5% response rate we need to target a very large market so we can receive a large response. If we only have a market consisting of 100 potential customers our response rate will only be 5 people. Unless you are selling a $10,000 item, which I doubt you are, you need allot more customers. You need to be targeting at least 1,000,000 people so when only 5% of the people respond you will have a great deal of customers. Five percent of 1 million people is 50,000 people, which I am sure you can agree is allot better than only five customers. The question is how to ensure that you have the opportunity to reach 1,000,000 people.

Reaching 1,000,000 people is not as easy at placing an ad in a large circulation newspaper. There are many newspapers and magazines with circulations of over 1,000,000, but placing an ad in is not a guarantee that you will reach them all. Sounds strange? When you think about who reads a magazine you will realize that they are a diverse crowd with different interests ranging from cooking to reading to exercising. So even though they all might read your ad they will not respond unless the ad interests them. The five percent response rate is only based on people who would be inter-

ested in the product you are offering. If only 1% of the people
reading a magazine are interested in your product then only 5% of
that 1% will respond to your ad. On the other hand if all the
readers of the magazine are interested in your ad you will then
have a response rate of 5% based on all of the readers.

The answer to the question on how to reach as many people as
possible is by ensuring that your product appeals to a wide base of
people. A classified ad selling earrings will only appeal to women
who wear earrings. On the other hand, a classified ad that sells
socks will appeal to everyone who wears socks, which is pretty
much every single person. When you advertise a product that appeals to everyone regardless of their personal interests you will have
a very good chance of selling a very large number of products. The
reason is because when you sell a product that everyone needs
then every person who sees your ad is a prospect for it. But if the
ad only appeals to a few people your response rate will only be
based on those few people.

Sell products that appeal to everyone. Imagine if you could
sell the immortality, every single person in the world would become your customer. While you cannot sell immortality, there are
many products that appeal to everyone.

CHAPTER 16

How To Measure Consumer Demand

Before we can sell a product that has a very wide appeal we need to be able to find out which products are bought by everyone. Once we have determined which products have the largest appeal we can secure a source from where to buy tit and start selling it. I will now teach you how to be able to determine which products have the largest appeal.

The most effectual way to ascertain the product with the largest appeal is to look within our own homes for the answer. Make a list of which items you and your family all use. Some of the products on your list should be hygiene products, food, and vitamins. You can sell toothpaste knowing that everyone uses toothpaste and will buy from you if you can offer him or her top quality brands at discounted prices.

If you think about everyone you know you will realize that everyone shares certain interests regardless of their personalities and status in life. There are certain needs that are standard in all people. Some of these needs are the desire to be healthy, to be attractive, to be make more money, and the list goes on. If you can provide a product or service that caters to one of these needs you will have a potential customer base consisting of every person on this planet. You can capitalize on these needs by selling products that enable people to fulfill their needs.

You can help people fulfill their need to have more money by selling information on how to start a business. You can fulfill the need of people to be healthy by selling vitamins and healthy food recipes. If you are unsure how to exactly fulfill those needs ask yourself what someone could sell you to fulfill your needs. Chances are that what ever would fulfill your needs will also help other people fulfill their needs. You can use yourself to figure out what the best products are to sell to people. I am sure that you have the desire to make more money. Think about what someone could give you to help you make money. It could be advice, a source of products, an advertising directory, or a book teaching you explicitly how to start a business. You would buy that information if you believed that it could help you make money. You need to reverse the situation. This time there are other people who are looking for ways to make more money. You want to offer them the information that you would be willing to purchase to help you make money. Since you will be directly helping to fulfill a need you should have a nice response rate.

Another need is based on people's desire to improve. They want to feel better and have more energy. This feeling is very common among people who have undergone a tough period in their lives and now want to hit the ground running and be back to their old selves. Elderly people are also always looking for the right nutrition so they can continue to be as active as they desire. Pregnant women also need to stay healthy and be careful with what they eat since they are eating for two. Pregnant women and nursing moms also constitute a big market that is need of healthy food and vitamins. Athletes are always looking for the right supplements to provide them with the extra energy that they need to compete. Weightlifters are always looking to ensure that they eat the appropriate food to help them build muscle mass. Children need to eat right so they can develop properly. I think you can see how virtually everyone is need of healthy food and vitamin supplements. If you sell healthy food, food recipes, or vitamins, you will be tapping into a market consisting of virtually every person in this country.

CHAPTER 17

Your Name Says It All

The name of your business is very important since it will instantly tell people what you do. A business with the name Lowy Wholesale Socks tells the world that the business sells socks at wholesale prices. A business with a vague name such as Lowy Ventures does not send a clear message to potential customers. You want to have a name that sends a very clear message to consumers as to the nature of your business. This way if a customer comes across your business name he will instantly know what the nature of your business is. This way if he is in the market for your product or service he will contact you. The same customer would not have the time to investigate a business with a vague name to see if it sells what he needs. If you were looking for watches and were flipping through a directory and found two businesses, one called Beverly Luxury Watches, and the other one, Timothy Inc., which one would you call?

The importance of the name is also based on the message that it sends to the customer. In Mail Order, the name is especially important because customers are judging you based on your ad. If your ad is a classified ad it will be indistinguishable from the next classified ad. If you want your business to stand out from among other classified advertisers you will need to use a name that sounds prestigious. A generic name will not work because everyone is used to seeing generic names springing up in classified ad sections.

Instead if your business has a name that conveys trust and

stability it will stand out. Compare a name like National Opportunity Books to Joe's Books. When you add the word National the business automatically seems to have more substance.

CHAPTER 18

The Importance Of The Right Address

Having the right address for your business is more important than the name of your business. The name of the business will influence how people think of your business but will not have the effect of the right address. People know that a name can be randomly selected and will not always reflect the actual business. A business addresses does say allot about the condition of the business. Since a business address can range in cost and can be very expensive the address that it uses means something. A business renting office space in a busy business district will pay as much as five times the rent that an office will pay in a less prestigious area of the city. The business that can afford to rent office space in an expensive area has money and is more than likely an established business. A fly by night operation would not rent space in an expensive area because they will have to pay at least two months upfront and sign a one-year lease. A landlord in a less desirable area who is struggling to attract renters will be more flexible to accommodate a potential tenant.

In addition a tenant in a less desirable area is usually not as economically secure as a tenant in a less desirable neighborhood. This is because a business with limited funds needs to resort to finding cheaper space even though it knows that it will attract less business by being there. Every business knows that the area that it is located in will be a reflection on its image; therefore no one would locate their business in an undesirable area unless they had no choice. I will show you how to locate your business in a desirable location without having to spend allot of money.

Many Mail Order businesses start out by using mailbox because of its low cost. You can rent a mailbox for as little as $6 a month. The use of a mailbox is a great way to get started since you do not have spend allot of money renting an office space and you can avoid having to give out your home address. The last thing you want is people showing up at your house looking to buy the products you are selling.

The problem with using a mailbox is that allot of people associate mailboxes with fly by night companies. They rationalize that anyone can rent a mailbox and simply take their money and run. Since all they have is a mailbox address they cannot track down the business if they do not receive what they ordered. Because of the potential abuse that could be done with post office boxes many people have shied away from responding to any ads that use them. The post office has remedied this situation by demanding identification from all renters. This way if any fraud takes place the post office can easily contact the owner of the mailbox.

Although the post office has taken very strict measures to ensure that fraud is not performed people are still reluctant to send money to mailbox. If you are determined to use a mailbox you can take the following steps to ensure that people feel secure enough to respond to your advertisement. You can send out information for free so people realize that they have nothing to lose by responding to your ad. After they respond you can them mail them your offer or catalog. Once they have your offer in their hands they will start to realize that you are not a fly by night operation. The extent of trust they convey to you will also depend on the quality of material you mail out to them.

Another way to ensure that people feel comfortable responding to your mailbox is by including a phone number through which they can contact you. You can set up an 800 number with recorder message. This way people will call the 800 number and be able to hear more information about your offer. You can leave a 30 second recorded message about your company and the product you are sending. Once people have an opportunity to gather more information about your company they will be more eager to respond to your offer. You can even use the recorded message to give them an address to which they can mail out the payment for your offer. The address you give them can be the mailbox since at this point they will know more about you and will be more inclined to sending you money if they are interested in your offer.

You can also use your ad to supply them with the address of your web site so they can log on to the Internet and read up on you and your company. The web site should also have the same advertisement so people can order if they like what they read. The key is to offer as much information as you can so people can trust you and realize that you are not a fly by night operation.

You can avoid the challenges of using a mailbox by using a real business address. I can assure you that people will be impressed if they see that your Mail Order business uses a real address instead of a post office box. They will realize that you are a real operation with real offices instead of just someone working out of their basement. I know that you probably do not have the money to rent an office at this point or you would already be in business. That is why I am going to show you a legal and profitable way to use a real business address without having to rent an office.

There are many private companies that are set up to rent out virtual offices to entrepreneurs who work from home. For a fee of as low as $10 a month they will allow you to use their address as your return address. They will accept your mail for you and keep it on a shelf until you pick it up. The cost of this service will vary by the level of mail you use but the prices are usually very reasonable. And anyways, if you are receiving thousands of orders you will be able to easily afford an extra $10 a month. The cost of using the private services of these firms is also influenced by the prestige of their address. A firm that is based in the World Trade Center will charge allot more than a firm based on a random street in Manhattan. I have used a firm located on a regular avenue and street. The advantage was that the total cost for the year of using their services was only $100, or $28 more than a post office box would have cost me. The same service from firm based in the Empire State Building would have sot me $75 a month, or $900 for the year. My business address was still prestigious since it was based in NYC and was based out of a real office. Anyone who read my ad would come to the conclusion that my business was based out of real offices and would be more inclined to place an order.

Every city has firms that will offer to accept your mail for a small monthly fee. Remember that all fees in life are negotiable and you can arrange a further discount by renting the box for 6 months or a full year. Only negotiate in person since they will realize that you are serious about renting their services, instead of just being an anonymous caller shopping around. Also when they see you come in person to their offices they will be more motivated to make sure that they obtain your business before you leave.

If you live in a neighborhood that lacks this type of a firm you can still rent an address in another city. You can call a firm and tell them that you are interested in renting out their services if they can forward all of your mail out to you. They should be willing to mail out all of your mail to you once a week if you supply them with stamps. This way for an extra $5 a month you can receive all of your mail without having to drive out to pick it up. If you use a firm that will forward your mail you can then use a firm that is located anywhere in the country. I know of one mail-forwarding firm located in Chicago with customers all around the country. This way even if your business is based in Nebraska your return address can be in the business district of Chicago.

Another approach is to use your own home address and let people know that merchandise is not kept on premises. This way people will not show up to your house with money ready to buy the merchandise.

Make sure that the address you use sounds prestigious and respectable. The difference in orders you can receive from using a prestigious address will be worth the extra cost.

CHAPTER 19

Select The Product You Will Be Selling

Now that you have learned how to set up the infrastructure of your Mail Order business you are ready to select the product that you will be selling. The decision on the product that you will be selling should be based on your own interests. The product or service that you offer should be one that you are familiar with and interested. This way you will know what would motivate someone to place an order. Also if you are a user of the product or service you will know what it is that people are looking for. For example, if you enjoy wearing hats you will know which hats are made of the best quality. You will be able to sell hats that people are interested in buying since you can base the selection of hats on your own fondness for them. If you enjoy wearing cotton sports hats you will be able to tell which hats are made of the best quality and which hats will sell the best. If you would not buy a particular hat, chances are that other people will not want to buy it. But if there is a hat that excites you and you would want to buy yourself, chances are that there are other people out there who would also like to buy the hat.

You might enjoy collecting comic books as a hobby. You would know which comic books are special and which ones are considered to be collectibles. You can use this information to buy and sell the hottest comic books. If you are unfamiliar with the comic book market it will be much harder to determine which comics will sell the best. Your hobby might be collecting stamps, records, antiques, cars, posters, postcards, books or toys. You can turn your knowledge of your hobby into a gold mine by selling to your fellow collectors by mail. You will have many loyal customers if you can offer them the collectibles they are looking for at low prices and at the quality they are looking for. If you look at comic book, antique, or baseball card magazines, you will see hundreds of dealers selling collectibles by mail. They are only selling through the mail because they know how much money they can make selling to collectors.

Selling collectibles by mail is an incredibly profitable business that can yield you thousands of dollars a week. You can buy collectibles for a fraction of their value at garage sales, flea markets, and moving sales. You can then turn around and sell them for as much as 10 times what you paid for them. You are able to buy the collectibles for so cheap because you are buying from people who do not realize what the value of their collectibles is. You can then mark up the collectibles since you are selling to collectors who are desperately looking for the collectibles you have.

You can start by placing a cheap classified ad in a magazine or newspaper catering to the collectible market. The cost of the ad can be as low as .25 a word. Your best bet when placing a classified ad in a collectible publication is to offer a free catalog and describe what differentiates your catalog from the rest. Collectors will be used to seeing hundreds of offers for free catalogs so they will hesitate to pay for one unless they are convinced that your catalog is different than the rest. You can charge for the catalog if you can convince collectors that your merchandise and prices are truly outstanding. You will need to spell out in a few words the highlight of your catalog. You could tell collectors that you deal with scarce collectibles at below price guide prices. Or you can indicate that you wholesale collectibles to the general public. The point is to send a message to collectors that it is in their best interest to send a few dollars for your catalog when they could instead obtain plenty of free catalogs from other dealers.

Your ad could read: "Comic Book Catalog of rare and sought after comics at 50% below price guide prices. Send $1 to Comic Book Inc. 1123 Marvel St LA CA 11111."

Using this ad you are letting collectors know that you carry hard to find comics at a 50% discount to the regular prices. You could solicit an even better response if you listed a few items that you carried and offered an even better discount.

You could use the same technique to make money by selling baseball cards through the mail. You can find thousands of baseball cards for less than a nickel each at local flea markets. Once you find and buy baseball cards you should buy a price guide and sort through the cards and write down a value for each one of them. I would not be surprised if many of the cards that you buy at flea markets are worth a few dollars each. Even if the average card you have has a value of .50 you can sell it for .20 and still make 4 times your money. The way you would do this is by buying 1000 cards for $50 and then selling the entire lot for $200 plus $5 for shipping. Your profit on the cards is $150. You can use the proceeds from the sale to buy 4000 more cards at .05 each. You then turn around and sell them through the mail for .20 each bringing in $800. You can keep doing repeating this process until you are buying and selling $5,000 worth of cards each time. You can make even more money by charging a few dollars for the handling of the cards. If the shipping charge is $5 you can charge an extra $2 for the handling of the cards. That extra $2 might seem small but when you realize that in the course of one year you can mail out 1000 orders you will realize that it will add up.

For years I bought and sold comic books at conventions and through the mail. I was able to buy comic books for as low as.06 each by carefully looking for bargains. I would look at the classified ads for merchandise and would see if anyone had any comic books they wanted to sell. I would often people with a few thousand comic book sitting in their garages. They would be more than happy to get rid of them and get a few bucks for them. I once had a man approach me and ask me to buy his comic books. His wife wanted to clean up their apartment and wanted the extra room his comic books were taking up. I told him that I might be interested but that I would need to take a look at them. He agreed but told me that since he had over 7500 comic books it would be hard to bring them all at once. I ended up buying them all over the course of a week for as little as .05 a comic. I turned around and eventually sold half of them for prices ranging from .20 a comic to as high as $5. I must have sold over 2000 comics for at least.50 each, 1000 at .50, a few hundred at $1, and a few more at $5 bringing in about $1800. And I still had at least 3,000 more comics to sell. Since my total cost was $600 and the proceeds from selling the comics was $1800, I made $1200 in profits. I can still the rest of the comics at .25 each and make an extra $800 or wait a littler longer and try to sell them for a $1 each and make another $3500. I also bought another deal of valuable comics from a dealer with excess comics for about .08 each. I bought 20 boxes of comics from him and sold them for as much as .50 each.

You can make even more money by selling comics through the mail to individual collectors. If you take the time to sell the comics individually you can charge as much as $25 for each comic. The next time you are around a comic book shop take a look at the prices that they are selling the comic books for. You will then see how much money you can make if you buy the comic books at the right price. You can contact me at Legacytrader@aol.com and I will be more than happy to help you locate comic books for less than .25 each. Or you can attend garage sales and flea markets and start bargaining.

If antiques are your cup of tea you can also attend garage sales and flea markets and resell the treasures you find for many times more than what you paid for them. I know one enterprising couple that love finding old antiques at garage sales. They use their keen abilities to detect promising antiques that need some restoration. They buy them and clean them up to the point to which the original owner would not recognize the antique. I once saw them buy a beautiful marble chess set with a value of over $200 for only $5! The chess set was old and dirty and needed a good cleaning. Once they were finished cleaning it the chess set resembled a museum piece.

You can find and buy great antiques at flea markets for as little as 1% of their true value. You can then clean the antiques and sell them through the mail for as much as 125% of their value. The reason that you can sell antiques for as much as 125% of the guide value is because collectors are willing to pay very high prices for items that are unique. For instance, a painting might have a price guide value of $1000 but a collector could be willing to pay over $1000 if he has spent years looking for it. The more he likes it the more he will pay.

There are many items that you can easily sell through the mail with the use of catalogs. Take a picture of the item and include it in your catalog along with a small description. Always include a full guarantee so your customer will feel comfortable paying a high price for an item that he cannot examine ahead of time. You should strongly recommend your customers to include a payment for insurance in case the item is damaged during shipping. I believe the post office charges $1.50 per ever $100 of value being shipped. I always insure all the orders I mail out so I can quickly resolve any situations in which the item arrives damaged.

Another very profitable product that can be sold through the mail is information. Information sells so well because people are always looking for a way to improve their lives. They want to improve their homes, health, financial condition, and their social life. In addition to wanting to improve their lives people are always looking for something new. They want something new to break the mundane routine that life often takes. You can supply them with the information that they can use to change their daily routines. They type of information that can change the daily routine is information on starting a business or on traveling. You can offer people detailed instructions on how to start and grow a successful business that can change their lifestyles. The appeal of starting a business is so high because of what starting a business promises. Once you start a business you are taking steps to move away from living paycheck to paycheck and instead you are positioning yourself to be more in control. No one likes having to report to a boss or to depend on someone else for a paycheck. By nature people want to be independent and they are always looking for a way to be more independent. I am sure that you have noticed that the people who enjoy their jobs enjoy a great deal of independence. The more they the ability to make their own decisions the more they will like their jobs. This is because people by nature want to be able to make their own decisions. You can help them come closer to being able to make their decisions when you show them how to start their own business. If you can demonstrate that the information you are selling them will allow them never to have to work for someone else again they will respond to your offer.

A similar principle helps information on traveling be such a good seller. Although many people want to break their daily routine by leaving their jobs, they are prevented from doing so. They cannot leave their jobs because of the financial obligations they face. Even though they might know that once they start a business they will make more money than in their jobs they are reluctant to leave their employers. This is because they are not ready to face the risk of leaving the security of a steady paycheck. The people in this situation will need something else to help them break their daily routines. Since they will not partake in the thrill of starting a business they seek another type of change.

The change you can offer them is the opportunity to travel. People love to get away and vacation. They would love the opportunity to temporarily leave their jobs and relax on a warm beach. But the reason that they do not pick themselves up and take off is because they cannot afford the high costs of traveling. But what if you could show them where and how to travel for well below their budget?

You can compile a list of vacation spots that cost under $50 a day to travel to. Your list can include the names of beaches that are often overlooked and can provide a high level of tranquility and enjoyment. For instance, while everyone is familiar with the expensive vacation spots in Miami and Hawaii, how many people know of all the beaches located in New Jersey, North Carolina, South Carolina, New York, and Massachusetts?

Instead of having to spend hundreds of dollars to fly out to a well-known tourist area you can drive a few hours and arrive at a beautiful unknown beach. You can write a short booklet teaching people how to save money by visiting vacation spots that are rarely publicized. People will love to pay you as much as $25 for your information if it can save them hundreds of dollars in vacation costs. Many people will not even be able to afford any vacation without reading your information.

Your information will allow hundreds of thousands of people to be able to afford to take vacations. You can obtain free listings of hotels across the country and then compile small booklets based on geographical areas and sell them. You can have one booklet for hotel accommodations, another booklet for cheap traveling tips, and another booklet for the best places to visit.

You can sell booklets based on the seasons. During the summer season you can sell an all-inclusive booklet for beaches. During the winter season you can make a booklet containing a list of inexpensive sky resorts along with rating information on each one. The possibilities are endless since there are millions of people who travel each month and are always looking for new places to visit. Think of all the booklets you can sell in one city alone based on only one advertisement.

The desire to travel is rooted in people's desire to explore and experience new places. They want to break the routine of life and bring some excitement in. Your booklets should cater to this desire by promoting the excitement of traveling. Instead of advertising a list of attractions you should advertise what people can do at the attractions. If you were advertising a list of beaches you would advertise based on what people can do at the beaches. You would list activities like swimming, snorkeling, fishing, jogging, and sailing. People want to go away not for the sand but for what they can do at the beach so you need to stress the activities that they can enjoy at the beach.

Finding information on your booklet should be very easy if you know where to look. You can log on to the Internet and do a search for tourist attractions in a given area and then print out a list of them. You can then do search for motels in the same area and include that list with your list of attractions. The final step would be to search for cheap modes of transportation. One of the cheapest and most overlooked modes of transportation available is the train. Amtrak offers train service all over the country for a fraction of the cost of purchasing an airline ticket.

To get a picture of the size of the travel market open up a newspaper and look at all the advertisements for hotels, airfares, and cruises appearing daily. You can capitalize on this market by focusing on selling publications tailored towards travelers. You would use advertisements placed in the travel sections of newspapers and travel magazines to promote your products and services.

I know of a company that sells books written specifically for travelers. Each book focuses on one country and contains all the information a traveler will need to know about local customs, safety, weather, and places to sightsee. The company has published and sold millions of copies to travelers who have come to rely on this information to prepare for their trips.

You can gain success by imitating their service and selling small reports on travel destinations within the United States. Your reports should contain all the information a travel might want to know about the place before he or she arrives. The books sell for over $10 so you know that people are willing to pay for travel information. This means that you can also charge $10 for your booklet if it contains enough applicable information. The quantity of pages is not what matters but it is the quality of information that is important. So if you can discover hard to find information that can make someone's trip even more exciting you should be able to charge a premium.

I want to return to the opportunity of selling business information through the mail. I know that you agree with me when I say that there is a tremendous amount of demand for information on how to start a business. Most people are divided into two categories when it comes to starting a business. There is one group of people who know what it is that they wan to do but do not know how to proceed and there is the other group that wants to start a business but need an idea on how to make money.

The first group could consist of people who want to go into Mail Order but do not know what steps they need to take to be successful. The second group could consist of people who have plenty of experience and knowledge and are now looking for a business opportunity that they can be involved in. They know how to advertise and how to market but they are looking for a product to market. You can sell thousands of dollars if information to each group if you know how.

The first group of people consists of people with drive and determination who want to work in a business and are looking for operating information. They will purchase books and magazines that can guide them in the process of running their businesses. You can sell them booklets on how to advertise, how to market, how to find products, how to set up their order tracking system, and many other types of booklets. They are looking for explicit instructions on how to run their business.

The second group posses many of the skills that the first group is looking for. But what they lack is an idea on what to do. They know how and where to advertise but they are looking for a product to advertise. They know how to run a business but are now looking for a new business to start. You can sell to this group of people information on specific businesses that they can start.

Picture this group of people as individuals who have a great of experience in the corporate world and now want to be in business for themselves. They have asked their neighbors and friends on suggestions for starting a business but have come up empty. If you advertised a booklet that would give list 50 businesses that they can start they would buy it because it would provide them with the information they are looking for. You could suggest to them that they should start a Mail Order business and offer to share with them in a booklet all the different products and markets that are available. Remember that they are looking for an answer to the question of, "What kind of a business can I start?" If you can provide that answer to them you should have plenty of business.

You should start out by writing down every type of business you can think of starting. Then divide that list into different categories according to costs involved, necessary experience, and business classification. You can then sell a list of businesses according to the divisions that you have made. You can sell a list of 10 businesses that you can start for under $100, another list of businesses in the food industry, and another list of businesses that require no experience. You can further divide and sell your lists according to smaller categories like businesses that can be started by one person, businesses that require part time help, businesses that sell hot food, businesses that sell cold food, businesses that can be started for under $1000, $500, or $100. The more refined your list is the more you will have to offer to people looking for clear choices for starting a business.

You can sell business information in business magazines geared towards those who are starting a business. There are many business opportunity magazines that are read by individuals who are looking for information on starting a business. Once they pick up that magazine they have clearly made themselves into a prospect. The only reason they would pick up a business opportunity magazine is because they would love to have more money by running a business. And since you want to advertise directly to people who have already demonstrated an interest in starting a business these types of magazines would make the best places to advertise.

You can also consider tabloid publications that reach a wide market. A national tabloid can have a circulation of over 2,000,000 readers. The entire readership of the publication might not be interested in starting a business. But once you place an ad in a large circulation magazine you will have a good chance of catching the attention of the few hundred thousand readers who are interested in making more money. Let us assume that only a quarter of the readers want to start a business, you will still have 500,000 readers. That number is higher than most business opportunity magazines can deliver with the exception of some of the well-known names like Entrepreneur, Inc, and Success.

To summarize, by advertising your business information in a national publication you are placing your ad in front of an immense readership. When you place your ad in a business opportunity magazine the readership is smaller but all of the readers have an explicit interest in starting a business. All of the readers of a business opportunity magazine are prospects for your offer while only a percentage of the readers of a national publication are interested in what you have to sell.

You can decide which medium of advertising is more effective for you by placing an ad in a tabloid and another ad in a business opportunity magazine. Have each ad use a different department number in the mailing address so you can tell which ad you receive the biggest response from. Both ads will have the same mailing address with the exception of a department that is meaningless. The purpose of the department is only to tell you from which ad the response has come from. This way you can measure your response rate by looking at the mailing address people used when they place orders. You will run a tally of all the orders each department received. If one department receives more orders than the other departments you know that the ad that uses it is doing the best for you. If everyone is sending in their orders to department number 25, then the ad that uses department 25 has the highest response rate.

Another great product to sell through the mail is electronics. Electronics are good products to sell through the mail since people do not need to see them to know what it is that they ordering. Everyone knows what a Zenith VHS VCR looks like. If they need more information on it they can walk into any electronics store to look at it and then decide who has the better price. To help shoppers locate information on what you are selling you will want to list the model number of the merchandise you are selling. This way they can log on to the Internet and read about the product you are selling. Once they have obtained information they can purchase it through you. In order to make sure that you are able to convince customers to buy you will need to compete based on price. Since electronics is a line of products that is easy to obtain consumers will make their decisions based on price. You are not selling a product that is hard to obtain so you need to encourage the customer to buy from you opposed to the other sources he can buy from. The way to encourage him to buy from you is by first shopping around and determining what the standard price is for what you are selling. Once you have determined the going price for what you will be selling you need to ensure that you have a source of supply that will allow you to establish a decent profit. Since you will want to sell electronics for at least 50% below retail you need to ensure that you can buy them for below wholesale. The reason you want to sell electronics for at least 50% below retrial is so you can stand out from all the other electronic retailers. There is an immense amount of competition from online and retail sellers so you will have to offer prices that will instantly distinguish you from the rest of the players in the market.

You can sell at 50% of retail and still double your money as long as you are able to buy for at least 50% below wholesale. This is not as difficult as it sounds if you are willing to put in the necessary effort. Your first step in locating merchandise at below wholesale is to contact Closeout Brokers who deal in electronics. They can offer you prices of as low as 25% of retail. You can obtain a list of Closeout Brokers by conducting a search on the Internet. Call them and introduce yourself to them and tell them exactly what it is that you are looking for. Within a few hours you should get a few offers from them for what you are looking for.

You can also obtain electronic merchandise by contacting Surplus dealers. A Surplus dealer buys excess merchandise from manufacturers for as low as 5% of the wholesale price. He will usually look to resell it for as much as 25% of the wholesale price. This means that a Surplus dealer might buy 1000 TVs for 10% of the wholesale cost. If the televisions have a retail price of $100 and a wholesale cost of $50, the Surplus dealer would have paid $5 for each set. He will then look to sell them for $12.50, and will offer a further discount depending on how many you buy. Assuming that you buy 500 of them for $10 each, your total cost is $5,000. You can now sell them through your Mail Order business at 50% of the retail price, or for $50 each. At $50 each you will gross $25,000 and net $20,000. If you are not ready to spend $5,000 on merchandise you can start out by only buying 20 TVs and as your business grows you can buy in larger quantities.

Surplus dealers and Closeout Brokers are a great source of all types of merchandise at below wholesale prices. If you need more information on locating below wholesale merchandise feel free to email me at legacytrader@aol.com.

Once you have located and bought electronics you can market them through a homemade catalog. The catalog can consist of only one item and be one page long. People might even be more willing to look at the catalog if its only page long since they can quickly look at what you have offer without having to flip through page after page. You can advertise the catalog in classified ads using the phrase, "Electronics at Wholesale Prices."

You can also use display ads to sell the electronics directly without the use of a catalog. The display ad should be placed in a magazine that has a readership base that has been proven to order from the mail. The advertising department of the magazine should tell you if their readers place orders directly from ads placed in the magazine or if they prefer to order from catalogs.

The best place to place advertisements for electronics is in publications that have other electronic related advertisements. You know that these publications must be good places to advertise since other more experienced businesses are advertising electronics. If their ads would not be producing sales they would not continue to place ads. If you want to take things one-step further, you should use their advertisements as inspiration for your ads.

We know that their ads must be pulling in sales since the ads are being renewed. And if we know that the ads must be pulling in sales we can conclude that the ad is well designed and is appealing

OWY

to readers of the publication. If you can create a similar ad using the ideas behind their ad you should be able to have a good chance of producing similar results to the one's produced by their ad.

Make sure that you consult a lawyer to ensure that you do not violate any copyright laws. It would be wrong for you to copy their ad word for word and it might even be wrong to write a very similarly worded ad.

But I am sure that you can still figure out a way to use your own words and ideas to closely mirror a very successful ad. If the other ad uses the word "new", you can use the word "latest". If they use the image of a rabbit you can use the image of a squirrel in your advertisement. My point is not to copy their ad but to convey the same message that their ad sends out.

There are thousands of other products that you can specialize in. If you need more ideas for finding products you should contact trade associations and ask them for a list of their members. They can give you a list of their members and the products that their members sell. You would then contact the members on the list and request a wholesale catalog of products that you can resell. Manufacturers and wholesalers are always looking for new customers and will be happy to initiate a relationship with you.

When you contact them you should tell them that you are interested in small products that you can buy from them in large volume. You will do much better in Mail Order when you have a low priced product that you can sell in a very large volume. If the price is low for the product that you are looking to sell you will be able to capture the purchases of customers who are not 100% sure if they really need what you are selling. But because you will be selling the product for a low price they will buy since they are not taking much of a chance by purchasing the product. A customer will take a chance to purchase a novel for $5 since he does not have much to lose. But if the same novel were priced at $25 he would be reluctant to spend the money unless he really wanted to read it.

You want to encourage potential customers to buy from you by offering them low priced merchandise and merchandise that is priced exceptionally low when compared to other asking prices for it. You can choose to sell low priced items by establishing relationships with suppliers of low priced items like giftware, books, magazines, toys, videos, and music.

Or you can choose to focus on selling more expensive merchandise but at substantial savings to the regular prices. If you want to be able to sell merchandise at below the regular prices you will need to find sources of merchandise from where you can buy it for less than the wholesale price. We have already discussed two great sources for below wholesale merchandise. The two sources are Closeout Brokers and Surplus dealers. Another overlooked source for buying merchandise at a fraction of the wholesale price are manufacturers. The same manufacturers who sell their merchandise at the wholesale price will sell you their irregular production at a discount.

A sock manufacturer that sells socks at $6 a dozen will usually sell irregular socks at $3, or 50% below the wholesale price. The socks can be considered irregulars for many reasons so you need to inquire as to why they have received that label. If the reason were because the socks are one quarter of an inch smaller than the regular socks they would make a good buy. People will be wiling to buy these slightly irregular socks and save 50% of the retail price. On the other hand, if the socks are considered irregulars because they have a large hole where the heel should be you better stay away.

Irregulars are often great moneymakers because you can buy them for a fraction of their wholesale cost and sell them for close to the regular retail price. Sometimes you can even repair the merchandise so it no longer is considered irregular. This might be worth your time if it enables you to sell the merchandise for as much as 10 times what you bought it for.

Pants that are missing a button and have a few small holes could be sold for as little as $1 a pair. You can buy those pants, pay someone $1 to sow them up, and then resell the pants for $20 a pair. If you do the sowing yourself you can save $1 a pants and pocket the extra profit.

The nature of the manufacturing industry is that a certain percentage of merchandise will always be irregular. Manufacturers are waiting for you to approach them and buy their irregular production. They have no other use for it since they cannot sell it to their existing accounts. Their regular accounts would not be willing to pay the regular wholesale price if they know that they can buy slightly irregulars for below wholesale. For this reason manufacturers do not advertise their irregulars and have to wait for someone to approach them and make an offer.

Since the prices for irregulars are not written in stone it is up to you to negotiate and establish a fair price for both you and the manufacturer. Fairness will ensure that the manufacturer will want to continue to do business with you. Once you develop a relationship with a manufacturer you can ask him for an exclusive right to buy all of his irregulars. This way you are the only one with access to the merchandised. Your Mail Order business will build a reputation for being the only source for the irregular merchandise that you sell.

You can build a fantastic income by buying irregular socks and selling them through the mail since everyone needs socks and everyone is always looking for clothing bargains. You can buy 12 pairs of socks for as little as $3 and resell them for .80 a pair, or $9.60 a dozen. Since socks sell for about $1 a pair in stores you will be offering your customer a 20% discount while you will be making over 300%. This means that if you sell 1000 dozen pairs of socks through the mail every month you will make an annual profit of $79,200. It can even get better if you sell other related clothing items at the same time.

You can back sell merchandise to your existing customer base to increase your sales. If you customers buy athletic socks you can include with their orders an offer for dress socks. This way the customer has an opportunity to place another order when he or she receives their merchandise.

Make sure that all the merchandise that you sell is closely related to each other. You want your merchandise to complement each other so people will place orders for other items listed on your catalog. You can increase the size of your average order if you include an offer for other related merchandise. If your catalog consists of VCRs you should include videotapes since you know that the buyer of a VCR will want to purchase tapes so he can watch them on his VCR. A Mail Order dealer selling compact discs will want to include a listing of compact disc players for sale since the buyer of compact discs needs to have a compact disc player. Even if he already has a compact disc player he might want to place one in another other room or buy a better quality compact disc system for his home.

Your Mail Order business can take off if you insure that you can always offer your customers merchandise that is compatible with the merchandise that they are buying from you. A Mail Order business selling shoes would also want to sell shoe polish and shoe laces since everyone who owns shoes will have to at some point replace his shoe laces and polish his shoes. Although this piece of advice seems simple you would be surprised at how many people miss this lucrative idea when running their Mail Order business.

CHAPTER 20

Catalog Sales

Catalog sales are the lifeblood of many growing Mail Order businesses. The reason that catalog sales are so important is because they tend to bring in larger orders than advertisements bring in. The typical advertisement can only list a few products while a catalog can advertise a few hundred products. Instead of a customer making his decision based on only the one product being offered he can choose from hundreds of products.

While a person looking at an advertisement for a product might not like the color or size it is being offered in, he might still place an order if he saw a listing for the size and color he wants. Or the customer might not be interested in the product being sold but is interested in a related product. If he has a catalog in his hands he can still order a related product even if he is not interested in the featured product.

A catalog acts replaces the role of a store when it is in the hands of a prospect. The prospect can take his time and browse through the featured products and take his time deciding what he wants to order. Many prospects are not ready to order when they see an advertisement in the paper. This can be because they are used to shopping with someone else or want to get a second opinion before buying. By giving them a catalog to look at they can take the catalog and show it to the person who helps them shop or gives them advice on shopping. If your product is only featured on an advertisement you could miss out on their business since they not cut it out and save it.

An advertisement can produce sales but will not produce orders from shoppers who like to spend time looking at pictures and reading the descriptions while doing their shopping. To capture orders from these customers you need to be able to produce a catalog with well-written descriptions and clear pictures of the merchandise. One of the most successful catalogs in the market is the JC Penny catalog. It has full-page color pictures of the items along with full paragraph descriptions. This allows shoppers to study the pictures and imagine what they would look like using the advertised products. If you want to build a million dollar Mail Order business you should strongly consider using a catalog.

Today anyone can make a professional looking catalog using his or her home computer. There are many programs that will allow you to make documents using pictures that are already stored as files. You only have to open the file, select the picture that you want to use, and click and drag it to the place on the page that you want to put it. After you have placed an image in the page you can type in a short description of the item using the word processing program on your computer. After you have made enough pages featuring all of your products for sale you should print them out. You should then take the set of printed out pages to a local printer and have him make you a few hundred copies and collate them into a catalog. You will then have a professional looking catalog that is ready to be sent out to your customers.

If you want to use pictures of your items in the catalog you can also photograph your merchandise and place the photos on the printed out page. You then make a color photocopy of the printed out page with the color picture on top of it. The copy that comes out of the copy machine should look like the picture was printed on to the page. You can then take the copy and take it to a printer.

I once put together a comic book catalog using pictures that I had cut out from price guides and comic book magazines. I glued the pictures on to the page that I had typed out. I had written on each page a list of comic books that were for sale and glued a few pictures of other comic books on top of the page. I then made copies of each page and sorted them out into separate catalogs, which I could mail out, and hand to prospects.

If you are selling travel information you can use already existing pictures of the places that you are writing about. For instance, if you are putting together a booklet on Mexico, you can call the Mexican embassy and ask them to send you travel information on Mexico. You then cut out the pictures that they mail you and use them in your booklet. You need to make sure that you get permission to use pictures that you have not taken. To play it on the safe side you should inform the source of the pictures about your intentions. If your catalog can promote their business or aims they will want you to use their pictures so they can benefit at the same time.

Today, there are thousands of web sites on the Internet that allow users to download pictures for free and use them in any way they desire. You can obtain a list of these sites by conducting a search for pictures on the Internet using Yahoo or another search engine.

If your catalog sells information booklets you do not need to include pictures since what you are selling is the information and not the physical characteristics of the booklet. Most people are visually oriented so they will expect to see a picture of the item you are selling. If you decide not to use pictures for any reason you will have to compensate by making sure to write very clear and exciting descriptions of what you are selling.

An advantage that catalogs offer is that they can be saved and ordered from later. You can send someone a catalog in March and have him order from you a few months later. He could have tossed the catalog aside and found it a few months later on when he was cleaning up. If your ad had been in a newspaper it would have simply been thrown out. But since you used a catalog your "ad" can be saved for months.

Many people will save catalogs for special occasions like birthdays and anniversaries. They can see a product that they know that someone in their family will love and will hold on to the catalog until a special occasion. By providing them with a catalog you enable them to hold on to your advertisement until they are ready to order.

A catalog also allows a customer to place multiple orders. She might buy a sweater in December and a pair of gloves in February from the same catalog. She can pass on the catalog to her friends after she has used it. Your catalog can travel around gathering orders from people who you never even mailed it out to. Instead of only selling to the one person who has seen your ad in the paper you can sell through a catalog to many other people who are associated with the recipient of the catalog.

A mother in a family of five can place an order for everyone in her family when she sees what your catalog has to offer. If the same mother responded only to an ad for one product you would be limited to what you could sell her. At most, you could only sell her that one product instead of selling products to the rest of her family using a catalog.

The best part about a catalog is that it will continue to be a source of sales for as long as it is in circulation. The next part to make your catalog a success is to ensure that the catalog has what to offer. We have discussed how the prices must be well below the regular retail prices and how you must offer a variety of related products. We will know discuss how to assemble your catalog so as to produce the most sales.

CHAPTER 21

Catalog Design

The design of the catalog is crucial to creating a strong steady stream of sales from each catalog that you send out. The catalog needs to be designed in a fashion that will catch the attention of readers and encourage them to buy the products that are featured. The design will either encourage recipients to continue looking at its pages or to move on to another catalog. The average American family receives up to five catalogs in the mail every day. You have to distinguish your catalog by making it special enough for it not to be included in the recycling pile.

One way to make sure that the catalog is noticed is by including a note on its cover that the catalog is only sent to those whom request it. This message will remind the recipient of the catalog that he requested it and that it is not junk mail. You can even include the date the recipient requested the catalog on to refresh the memory of the recipient.

The cover of the catalog should have an announcement that would capture the interest of a lukewarm prospect. A lukewarm prospect is someone who is interested in the type of product you are offering but has not made a commitment to buy the actual product that you are selling. You can turn this prospect into a solid buyer by offering a deal that will knock his socks off. I would suggest including the following message on the cover of the catalog: "Last Month to save up to 80% off regular prices". Your catalog would then contain a list of the regular prices for the merchandise you are selling and the discounted price you are offering.

The reason you need to include this attention-catching message on the cover of the catalog is because when the prospect ordered the catalog he was probably very excited, but as time passed he might have lost some interest. You want to rejuvenate his enthusiasm by alerting him to a special deal. When he sees your special deal he will become excited again and take a good look at the catalog. The deal has to be exciting enough for him to want to open the catalog even if he does not remember having ordered the catalog.

There will be many times when you will mail out the catalogs to prospective customers who have not requested the catalog. For them to want to open up a catalog that they have not requested you will have to peek their curiosity. We all know the famous phrase of the cat and curiosity. To get prospects to open up your catalog and spend time reading it you will need to make them curious of what is inside.

You can also make them curious by having a unique cover design such as a famous painting or breath-taking picture. The name on the catalog will also make a difference. A name such as Jersey Watches is not exciting enough to get to people's attention. But a name like Royal Discount Watches tells people that the watches are fancy and are cheap. The name of your catalog is just as important as the name of your business. They both say allot about the type of business that you are running.

Besides a name for your catalog you need to have a slogan that people will remember. The slogan needs to be short and catchy so people will remember it easily. A great slogan for a watch catalog is "Time to buy time". The slogan refers to the benefit that buying watch provides, which is keeping time. The phrase will stick in people's minds because it contradicts that famous saying about not being able to buy time. The slogan you use should tell people what they are buying while entertaining them at the same time.

A logo is what keeps many billion dollars businesses in the mind of the public. And once you have implanted your logo in the consciousness of the publics mind you can use it to sell literally billions of dollars of merchandise. Mc Donald's uses its twin golden arches to sell its image to the millions of people around the world who eat at its fast food restaurants. Nike uses its swish logo to sell sneakers for as much as $150 a pair. People have come to associate the Nike logo with top quality athletic sneakers. When they see the logo they know that a company that promotes itself as the only source for top athletic sneakers and sport's wear has made the sneakers. If not for the reputation of Nike people would save their money and purchase sneakers for less than $20 from generic manufacturers. But because Nike has developed a reputation it can stick its logo ion any product and sell if for many more times the price than its competition can sell it for.

Your business will also develop a reputation as it proceeds in business. You should use a logo on all of your catalogs so people start associating your reputation with the logo. As your business grows you can capitalize on your reputation by letting other Mail Order dealers use your logo for a licensing fee. You can rent out your logo to other non-competing Mail Order merchants. Calvin Klein licenses out his name every year to clothing and accessory manufacturers who use its name and logo to sell their products. Your logo might have a following in the travel or business information industry that other people can use to promote their own businesses. If you rent out the name to them you can profit by either charging them a straight fee or by charging them a percentage of the sales they make using your logo.

You need to ensure that your logo becomes a popular symbol by including it in all correspondence and catalogs that you send out. If you use email include your logo on the email as part of the automatic signature. Place the logo on all display ads you use.

Once your logo and catalog name build a popular reputation you will be able to charge people to place their products in your catalog. Many Mail Order dealers and manufacturers will want the opportunity to be able to sell their products in your catalog. They will realize that there are thousands of people relying on you to buy high quality low priced merchandise so they will want to include their products. Just like you would be more prone to buy a product sold by a retailer with a high quality reputation, Mail Order customers also like to buy their products from catalogs with reputations for selling high quality merchandise.

You will have to make sure to carefully screen the manufacturers and Mail Order dealers who want to list their products on your catalog. Your customers will not distinguish between your products and other seller's products. Once the products are listed on the same catalog consumers make their decisions on the source based on what they obtained through the source.

It is worth allowing other sellers to list their products in your catalog since you can now make money from other peoples products. Instead of being limited to the 25 products that you have bought you can now have access to hundreds of products that you never had to buy. You can make money by charging a percentage fee or by marking up the prices that the other sellers want to receive and you keep the difference between what they asked for their products and what you actually sell the products for. You would set up a deal in which the seller of a product, we will use a video as an example, wants to sell his videos on your catalog. You would find out what price the seller want s for his videos and then mark up that price. So if the seller wants to charge $5 for each video you would list the video on your catalog for $8 each so you can keep the $3 profit. At this point you can also charge the seller of the video a 10% listing fee for the right to sell his products through your catalog. The seller will agree to this type of a deal because you are saving him the expense of having to advertise his merchandise, create a catalog, and mail it out to thousands of prospects. Since you have already made a catalog and mailed it tout to your prospects the seller knows that you have saved him the expense of printing and mailing the catalog. Also, if the seller does not sell any videos he has not taken any risk since he only pays you a fee based on a percentage of his sales. If you are considering taking on a product in your catalog that you are not sure of its potential you should charge the seller a small listing fee of $50 to

$200 to list his item and offer him a discount on the percentage of sales fee that you would get5 for selling his product. This way if the product does not sell you have still made money and the seller knows that you are going to give him a break by reducing the fee that you would charge on the merchandise that he sells.

Your catalog can entirely comprise of merchandise from other sellers. The advantage of creating a catalog consisting of offerings from other sellers is that you do not have to ship the items. The sellers would be responsible for shipping out the items that have been ordered while you would only be responsible for accepting and processing the orders.

You can charge sellers a premium based on the positioning of their product in your catalog. Since people have the most attention at the beginning the products that are listed in the first few pages will catch people's attention the most. You can also set your fee according to the size of the space that contains the listing and picture for the item that you are listing. The use of bold and extra large font in your catalog can also be used to distinguish one product from the next one.

You can make million soft dollars even using a catalog that consists entirely of your own products. In this case you would seek out sources for products and list them through your catalog. There are many ways to effective secure products that you can make allot of money selling. One way to secure products for your catalog is by attending auctions and bankruptcy sales. Auctions and bank-ruptcy sales are great sources of merchandise because the seller is usually facing financial difficulties and is desperate to raise cash. His desperation will lead him to allow the auctioneer to sell the merchandise for pennies on the dollar. The same thing takes place at a bankruptcy sale. The owner of the business owes money to his creditors who have now taken possession of his business. They know that they cannot recover the entire money owed to the so they will sell all of the assets for the business so they can recover even a small percentage of the money owed to them. If the bankruptcy sale brings in 20% of the money owed tom them it is considered a successful sale, so you can imagine how low the prices for the merchandise will be. I attended an auction in which $25 women's hats were sold for .25 each. The buyer of the women's hats can resell them for half price and make over $12 hat. His entire cost for the 400 hats was $100 and he can sell them all for a total of $4800 at half price or $10,000 for the full retail price.

There are amazing bargains available at bankruptcy sales that can yield you fantastic profits in your Mail Order business. At one sale that I attended 100 men's shorts were sold for .10 a piece! The shorts had a retail value of over $20 each. The buyer paid $10 for shorts with a retail value of $2,000. If he sells the shorts for 25% off the retail price he will gross $1,500 and net $1,490. At the same sale another buyer bought satin sport jackets with a retail price of $40 for only .50 each. That buyer positioned himself so he can make thousands of dollars when he sells the jackets.

Bankruptcy sales and auctions are listed every day in your local newspaper. Some newspapers, including the NY Times, have a full page devoted towards auctions once a wee. In the case of the NY Times, every Sunday there is a full-page ad in the back of the employment section full of advertisements for auctions that are taking place that week. The advertisements have a description of what is being sold, an approximate quantity of items being sold, and an approximate wholesale value of the merchandise. Most ads will have a combination of the previous descriptions and will always list the name of the auctioneer along with the address of the auction.

All you need to attend an auction is cash or certified checks. When you arrive at the auction the auctioneer will give instructions on hoe the auction will work and what you will need to do to claim the item that you win the bidding for. He will allow the bidders to walk around and examine the items and then proceed to start the bidding process. The bidding is done by lot and usually is done by the auctioneer picking up one sample and showing it to the bidders and giving a short description. You should only bid for items that you are familiar with and know the true retail price of the items. Many bidders get caught up in the auction process and bid more than they intended to so you should have a predetermined limit.

Auctions are great places to buy merchandise that you can resell in your Mail order business. At the same time you need to be careful that you do not buy someone else's junk, so make sure that you are sure that you can sell the merchandise and that your potential customers are interested in the items that you are considering buying. Once you decide what items you are interested in buying do not loose sight of it and make sure that you buy it by offering a bid that is below what you can sell it for. Many bidders give up an item just because the bidding has moved up below what they expected to buy it for. I have seen many bidders drop out of buying a $50 item just because the bidding has move dup from .10 to .25. This is quite foolish since if the item retails for $50 it should not matter if you buy it for .10, or even .50. Establish what the most you can pay for that item is and still be able to make the profit that you are looking for. At the same time make sure that you never pay the wholesale price since you can always contact a wholesaler and buy it for that price.

Bankruptcy sales also offer tremendous savings on the merchandise that is being liquidated. There will be allot of merchandise that is being sold for blowout prices so make sure that you do not merchandise that you do not need only because it is cheap.

All the items that you buy at bankruptcy sales and auction should be listed as specials in your catalog. You need to inform your potential buyers that the items are available in a limited supply and will be sold on a first come serve basis. By letting your customers know this you are creating a feeling of urgency to get them to buy now before the items are sold out. And because you cannot re order the items at the prices you paid for them you need to alert your customers to the fact that they should not expect to see them again, if they want to take advantage of your incredible prices they need to buy now.

We will now move on to discussing the actual lay out of the

catalog. The catalog should consist of the cover in the way we discussed in the beginning of the chapter. The cover needs to be eye catching and bright. It should use your own logo and slogan to build brand awareness. A phrase that conveys urgency and great savings must be included at the top of the cover. The purpose of the phrase is to let recipients of the catalog know that his catalog contains items that cannot be found in other catalogs and that it ids worth their time to look at the merchandise being offered.

The first page inside of the catalog should contain a welcoming letter introducing your business to the recipient of the catalog. In the welcoming letter you want to let them know what makes your catalog special and what type of merchandise to offer. You can use this letter to tell them a little about yourself and how many years you have been in business. If you are part of any trade groups or give money to any specific charity you can list it in this section. Finish off the letter by letting the readers know about your most special offer in that issue of the catalog. This way while you have their attention you can lead them straight into one the items that you are selling in the catalog.

The next section of the catalog should contain the items that are for sale including their pictures and descriptions. Each page should contain at most five small items or three large items. If you list too many items on each page people will get confused and set the catalog aside and move on. You want the catalog to be pleasing to the eye so it is easy to look at. Studies have shown that each page should have an expensive item, a cheap item, and a middle priced item. This way people will see the expensive item and will want to look for something cheaper. They will then see the cheap item and decide that they can afford to spend a little more and will settle on the mid priced item.

You can also advertise the items by sections using either price or another category to compose the sections. Your catalog can be divided by women's and men's products, or by cheaper, mid priced, and expensive items. I personally would prefer to see the sections separated by item category so I can turn to the section of items that I am interested in. At that point you should use then technique of listing three items priced differently. If you have a few hundred items to list what you should do is have a few small pictures of items on the top of the page and then on the rest of the page have a one description of each item. Each page would have a row at the top of pictures of the items followed by a page with item listings.

For example, your page could look like this:

*))))))))))))))))= %-% This is the place for your pictures.

Marvel Chess Set $19.99 Item # 25

Leather Jacket $49.99 Item # 26

At the bottom page you would inform the reader to place his order using the order form that is located on the last page. The order form should consist of columns for the name of the item, the item number, and the price. After the box where the customer fills in the total dollar amount of his order you should have instructions for adding in the cost of shipping and tax if any. You need to have a column for the name and item number to make sure that the customer did not write in the wrong number.

CHAPTER 22

List Your Items In Other People's Catalogs

You can save the cost of having to produce a catalog if you use other people's catalogs to sell your merchandise. You would start out by locating a source of products that you would like to sell. Once you have located a source for the products that you want to sell you have to decide in what type of a catalog your product would best sell.

A leather briefcase would sell in a catalog aimed at business people and professionals. You would want to list your merchandise in the catalogs that are being sent to the market that would be interested in buying your product. Start out by writing down what market your product should be sold at. Depending on your product there might be more than one market that it can be sold at. After you have decided to which markets you want to sell your product to you have to locate catalogs that serve that market.

Call up the companies and request their catalogs. Once the catalogs arrive look through them and see if your product would fit in with the other items being sold. If you find a catalog that you like and feel that it could help sell your product you would want to contact the buyer for the catalog. Call up the buyer and ask him what the process would be for him to evaluate you product. Tell him that you would like to sell your product in his catalog and would be willing to send him a sample if he is interested. When you send the sample enclose extra postage in the package so he can return the sample after he is done examining it.

If the buyer decided to carry your product in the catalog you will have to discuss a system in which you and them can make money by selling your merchandise. Avoid having to pay any listing fee and offer to give them a higher percentage of the gross instead.

The advantage of selling your product through someone else's catalog is that you will not have to go and find customers for your product. Your product will be brought to the attention of the customers of the catalog when it is featured in its pages. The catalog can be mailed out to thousands of current and potential customers. Those customers will now have an opportunity to buy your product without you having to spend nay money to print and mail out the catalog. Another advantage is that if you list your catalog in a well established catalog you can be assured that the people that it is mailed out to are serious customers who have either requested the catalog or have ordered from it in the past. Since you are only paying the catalog a percentage of your sales you will only be paying once you have sold merchandise. You can set your price according to the percentage that you will have to pay the catalog so you can establish your required profit.

An alternate to listing your item in a catalog is to advertise it as an insert in another publication. For a fee most newspapers and magazines will allow you to insert a one-page flyer in their publication. The flyer can be either black and white or color and the charge is usually higher for color inserts. The rates will also vary according to the circulation numbers of the publication. A local daily newspaper in a small town will have a much smaller circulation than a national tabloid and its rates will be comparatively cheaper. You can start out by testing your advertisement using an insert in a small circulation publication. If you receive a favorable response you can then pay to have the flyer inserted in a publication with a larger circulation.

The flyer should consist of an advertisement for your catalog along with a special sale on an item that will draw people's interest. The more appealing the sale on the item is the more people will order the catalog. It might even be worthwhile to sell an item at cost to encourage people to order the catalog so they can obtain further savings.

Be prepared that you should have enough merchandise available to fulfill all the orders that the flyer can bring in. A flyer placed in 100,000 copies of a newspaper can produce anywhere from 1 order to 100,000 orders so be ready to be surprised. If you receive too many orders for your product return the checks with a 25% off coupon for their next order. This way people will not be upset that they missed out on ordering that special item since they will be able to save 25% on their next order. To make sure that you are never out of stock for special item that you advertise contact the manufacturer or supplier of the item and ask them what their production capacity is for the item. Can the produce as many items as you are expecting to sell?

For this reason I like to sell items such as books. Books are easy to produce in any quantity as long as you give the printer enough advance notification. If the print run consists of 10,000 copies and you need more copies all you need to do is call the printer and order another few thousand copies. Or even better, if you are ordering directly from a publisher all you need to do is order more copies and they will ensure that they are delivered promptly. Certain publishers will have the books shipped directly to your customers and save you the work of mailing out individual copies to the thousands of people who order them.

Staple items like socks and food can also be easily produced. If your ad does not specify a brand name you can even order from another supplier if your current supplier runs out of stock. This way if you place an advertisement for chocolate cookies and receive an order for 50,000 boxes of them you can contact a few suppliers until you have put together enough boxes. If you are selling slightly irregular socks you can buy the socks from as many mills as you want since all of the socks are barely distinguishable and you have not offered one specific brand for sale.

One method that is popular among Mail Order dealers who do not want to make a catalog is post card advertising. Post card advertising is the practice of mailing out your offer on a post card to your prospects. You start out by purchasing list of potential prospects from a mailing list company. You then have the post cards printed at a printing shop at a cost of less than .02 each. You can them mail out 1,000 cards for less than $300 to the names on the mailing list that you have purchased. If the item that you are selling gives you a $15 profit and you receive a 5% response rate your total profit will be $750. Subtract your printing and mailing costs from your gross profit and your net profit will be $450, or 150%. When your Mail Order business build sup you will be able to send out 10,000 post cards instead of only 1000 and produce 10 times the amount of profits.

You can also pay to have a post card inserted in a card deck. There are marketing companies that send out decks of cards sealed in plastic to a few hundred thousand prospects. They will charge you a few hundred dollars to insert your post card in their deck of cards. But the investment can quickly pay off since they are sending out the deck of cards to over 200,000 people. For the same amount of money that it would cost you to send out a few thousand post cards you can now reach a few hundred thousand prospects.

Another advantage is that when people receive a singular post card in the mail they are likely to either loose it or miss it in the mail. But when a card arrives in a small package people will take the time to open up the package and look at what is inside. This way they will spend the time to flip through the cards looking for something that interests them. Once they see your card they can set it aside and decide if they want to respond to it. To make sure that they do respond to your card make it as easy for them as possible. You can provide information on how to receive a free catalog or provide a telephone number to which they can call to receive more information.

Answering services can be used if you do not want to give out your home number. The answering service will charge a small monthly fee and in return will answer all your phone calls in your company name. The operator reads the caller the information that you left the answering service and takes down the caller's information. You can mail out the customer the requested information or surprise him by calling him up and explaining your business to him yourself.

You can use a fax service that will allow the customer to call a number and enter his fax number. After he enters the number of his fax machine the fax service will automatically fax him the information that you have provided. This way the customer can receive the information without having to sit down and write a letter requesting additional information. In addition, by using this fax service the customer will receive the information within tow minutes instead of having to wait a few weeks to receive the information by mail.

The information that you include to be faxed to inquiring customers should consist of a short description of your business along with a few offers that the customer can act on. You want to turn every time you contact the customer into a sales opportunity. The information you fax to him will have an offer, the operator should let him know your latest offer, the post card should have an offer, and every piece of correspondence with the customer should have one.

You are in the Mail Order business to become a millionaire and in order to create a fortune in this business you have to take advantage of every opportunity to sell merchandise to your customer. Even the thank you letters that you send to your customer should have special offer to thank him for his business. Think about it, when your customer receives a sincere thank you letter from you for his business he will be happy and want to continue the relationship he has with you. At that point he is the likeliest to place another order so you want to give him the means and the excuse to place another order. The means is the order form you will send along with the thank you letter and the excuse is the special offer that you will be sending.

We will now discuss one of the favorite methods that successful Mail Order operators use to build their fortunes.

CHAPTER 23

Drop Shipping

Drop Shipping is the process of having your supplier mail the order directly to your customer. This process allows you to sell merchandise without having to worry about storing it and mailing it out. It also saves you the risk of buying merchandise that you might not be able to sell later on. A supplier who is willing to drop ship the items allows you to focus on advertising the item without having to spend any money on first buying the product.

For instance, you could sell collectible dolls that the supplier aggress to drop ship to your customers. In this situation you would advertise the collectible dolls and wait to receive orders for the dolls. Once you receive the orders you deposit the checks and money orders. You then write out a check for the price that the supplier charges for the collectible dolls plus the charge for shipping them. After the supplier receives payment for the collectible dolls he will send them out to all of the people on the list you gave him. This process is great since you keep the premium that you charge for the dolls and only send the supplier payment for the dolls once you receive orders for them. The supplier then worries about the shipping and ensures that every customer receives what he or she ordered. Instead of you having to order 1000 dolls and then trying to sell them you advertise the dolls that the supplier is selling. And instead of having to spend an entire day packaging and mailing the orders you can have the supplier do it for you.

Many people who run their Mail Order businesses as a secondary source of income sell products that can be drop shipped.

This way they do not have to spend time being involved with the packaging and shipping of the item. Also using a drop shipper allows them not to invest money in buying merchandise. You are basically the middleman (or woman) in the transaction. The best part is that the drop shipper will mail out the packages using your name and return address so the people who placed the orders will not try to order to order the products directly. You and only you appear to be the source for the marvelous products that they have ordered.

Your only cost when using a drop shipper is advertising. You have to pay for advertising to publicize the products of your supplier. I will show you in the next chapter how to advertise for free.

CHAPTER 24

Advertise For Free

You can advertise your product line for free. You can run your entire Mail Order business for under a hundred dollars when you use a drop shipper and you use free advertising. We discussed how a drop shipper enables you to avoid having to purchase the items from the supplier. Now we will discuss how you can eliminate your cost of advertising so you do not have to spend any money in either buying or selling your products.

One method of advertising for free that we have discussed is placing your product in catalogs. This way your product reaches consumers without you having to spend money producing your own catalog. The only cost to you will be the percentage of each sale that you pay to the owner of the catalog, but since that amount only comes from sales you would not have nay out of pocket expenses.

I will show you another way to advertise for free that can be quite effective when done in the right publication. This approach requires you to contact the advertising department of the publication you want to be in and set up a profit sharing deal. The profit sharing deal would give the publication a dollar amount for every unit that was sold through their publication.

The item that you would be selling would be advertised however they choose. They would be compensated either per unit they sold or on sliding scale. The more units they sell the more they would receive per item. This type of an arrangement will motivate them to place a nice sized ad that will attract serious attention instead of a small ad placed in the back section buried under the classifieds.

The arrangement that you would have with publisher will allow you to make even more money since you can obtain a large ad that is normally beyond your budget for free. The arrangement will also allow you to reach more people by having an ad in a large circulation publication.

I have come up with an example using numbers to show you how you and the publisher would benefit. Remember that you will be using suppliers that drop ship the ordered items. Here is the example:

You contact a publisher and offer to give him $2 for each $20 book that he sells through his advertisement. The supplier charges you $4 for each book so your profit per book is $14 including the $2 you will pay the publisher. The publisher agrees and places an ad that produces 2,000 orders for the book. The publisher receives the orders and makes a record of how many orders you received. He then sends you the orders along with a bill for how much he is owed. You then deposit the checks and write out a check to the supplier of the books. The supplier mails out the books to the customers and fulfills the orders for you. You then mail out $2 per book that has been ordered to the publisher of the advertisement. In this example you received $40,000 in orders. You have to send $8,000 of that money to the supplier and $4,000 to the publisher. You keep the rest as your profit. If you make a quick calculation you will see that your total profit is $28,000 and you never had to spend any money out of your own pocket. All the money that you paid to the publisher and to the supplier came straight from the money that came in from the orders. You can repeat this cycle in five different newspapers every two months. At that rate your total profits would be well over $800,000!

Even if you only make 25% of that amount you will soon be on your way to making a million dollars in your own Mail Order business.

CHAPTER 25

Classified Advertisements

Classified advertisements are the most inexpensive source of advertising for a Mail Order business. For a few dollars per word you can reach hundreds of thousands of eager prospects. Classified ads appear in the backs of thousands of magazines and newspapers. Pick up a sample newspaper or magazine and you will see that they are full of classified ads. There are classified ads selling all types of services and merchandise. These ads are read by millions of people who can potentially become your customers if you capture their attention.

Classified are easy to write. They are simple to place in any publication. Most ads are 10 words long and can be written by anyone with the most basic grasp on the English language. The ads are so easy to write because all you are required to write is the basic message that you want to deliver. You do not need to use any fancy wording to attract attention to your ad. The opposite is often true, the easier the ad is to read the more people will read it. If they understand the message of the ad they will be more prone to responding to your ad. Your ad can simply offer information on Mail Order and receive responses from people interested in learning more about Mail Order.

You will discover if you are persistent in using classified ads that they are a great source of revenue when used properly. There are many ways to effectively use a classified ad to produce a tremendous stream of revenue. We will discuss a few of the ways a classified ad can be used to help you skyrocket your Mail Order business.

The most important rule when using classified ads is to continue placing ads until the response rate builds up to your desired level. Studies have shown that it can take three times until an ad has an effect on people. If you want to succeed with classified ads you need to be persistent and place the ads for at least three recurring issues. And even then you will need to continue placing ads so people take notice of your advertisement. You would be surprised at how many people will start responding to an ad once they see it for the fifth time. Once they see the ad running for so long their curiosity will be picked and they will start rationalizing that the advertiser must have something of value if the ad is running so long and so many people must be ordering from it. If people were not ordering form it then the advertiser would not renew the ad?

You can create the same perception among readers of your publication if you renew your classified ads more than once. The most important thing is to be patient and not to give up if you do not see the orders rolling in right away. Keep in mind that people like to take their time placing orders and might respond to your ad a few weeks after having cut it out from the paper.

This time lag between people seeing your classified ad and ordering from it will matter less and less as you place more ads. This is because if you have been placing ads for the last few weeks and are still placing ads you will always be receiving a steady amount of responses from the ads that you placed a few weeks before. Four or five months down the road you can still be receiving responses for all of the classified ads that you have placed. Make sure that you always have a budget to place at least one classified ad per week. Your goal is to receive a steady amount of requests and orders a month after placing your first ad.

Classified ads are perfect for selling all types of information. Open up any newspaper and you will see classified ads selling all types of information. People from all walks of life are selling their experience in their occupations and businesses through the classifieds. You can join these Mail Order entrepreneurs and start selling your information through the mail.

The type of information that you sell is entirely up to you. All types of information can be sold ranging from recipes to business information. You can research any topic that interests you and sell it through the mail. You would start out by compiling information on the topic that you want to write about. You would then write a five to twenty five page report on the topic and sell it through the classified ads. It's really this is easy. You can have a printer print you 1000 copies of a 5-page booklet for a total of $250. You can then advertise the booklets using classified ads for $5 each. Look at the profits you would make if you sell 1000 five page reports for $5 each. The best part is that if you write a small page report you can easily print more copies as the orders arrive. You do not even have to print the booklets until the orders come in.

Classified ads really work in selling information. The biggest proof to how effective classified ads are is the abundance of classified ads selling information. If the ads were not reproducing sales people would not use them.

You can also use your classified ads to promote your catalog. You can charge a few dollars for your catalog. By charging people for your catalog you can establish that they are interested in purchasing from your catalog and not just collecting information. They would not pay for something unless they were serious about using it. The second benefit of charging for your catalog is that you can also make money by every time someone orders your catalog. If you charge $2 for each catalog you can make at least $1 per request since the catalog should not cost more than .50 to print and mail out, and the ad itself should cost under $100.

The more specialized the information the more interesting it will be to the readers of the classifieds. They are used to seeing hundreds of ads for broadly categorized information such as "How To Make Money" or "Start a Business". But there are very few ads offering very detailed information one specific type of business. How many ads have you seen with the following headline "Start a Video Rental Business From Home" or "Learn how to paint in 30 days"?

To maximize the response rate from your classified ads you need to offer something that no one else in the publication is offering. Use your imagination and you can come up with thousands of ideas that no one else has ever sold through classified ads. The effort is worth the reward when you think about how many prospects will be looking at your ads. The Enquirer has a circulation of over 1,000,000 copies, what if you received an order from every single reader? What if you only received an order from one out of every 10 readers?

You can make a tremendous amount of money using classified ads if you sell a product with a large demand that is unique and hard to find. One type of publication that sells well is a directory. People will are always looking for sources of products that they can resell. People seem to be willing to pay good money if someone can compile a directory of information for them.

There are Mail Order experts who feel that you should not charge in a classified ad. They feel that people will respond more often if they do not have to send in money to receive information or to receive a catalog. I feel that if you motivate people enough and show them in the classified ad how they can benefit from the information people will be willing to send in money. A classified ad is lie any other type of ad, the more interesting and appealing it is the more it will encourage people to respond. You should charge people to receive information or a catalog so you can separate between browsers and serious buyers.

The same applies to selling directly from a classified ad. While some experts feel that you should not sell directly from an ad I believe that you can sell directly from the ad as long as what you are selling costs less than $10 and seems unique and useful. You can play it safe by placing an ad that does not ask for money and an ad that does ask for money. Keep track of the people who respond to the free classified ad and see if they become customers later on. If they do not become customers you would have been better off without them since all that they did was request information because it was free. On the other hand, if they do order

from you later on it might be worth it to continue running ads
that do not ask for money. This is a number's business and you
need to compute which way you will make more money. I have a
strong feeling that you will discover that you will make money in
the long run by charging at least a dollar for any information or
catalog that you send out.

The best part of running classified ads is that they are cheap
so you can test out a multitude of ads until you discover the one
that yields the best results. You can run a series of ads from which
consumer can request free information and a series of classified ads
that require payment.

Before we move on to discuss the particulars of running a
successful classified ad campaign you need to select what you will
be selling with the classified ads. Once you have decided to select
a product that you want to sell, or a catalog that you want to
advertise, you need to find the proper publication. The publication
that you will be placing your ads in must cater to the audience
that is the most prone to buy your product. A catalog for business
opportunity information should be advertised in a publication with
a large audience of business opportunity seekers. A self help manual
can be advertised in a publication that people who are looking to
improve their lives would read. Publications such as national
tabloids are good places to advertise self-improvement and self help
information. Celebrity related information such as celebrity
addresses and celebrity information should be advertised in
publications that cover the lives of celebrities. Information on for
aspiring actors and actresses should be advertised in entertainment
magazines since many of their readers harbor dreams of becoming
actors.

The publication that you choose to advertise in should contain similar advertisements for the product that you are looking to
sell. A publication with many advertisements for a certain type of
product would tell you that the readers of that publication enjoy
buying that product.

If you are not sure what to advertise you can take the reverse approach. You can read the classifieds of the publication and see which products are advertised the most often. You will then know which products sell the best through the classifi9ed ads. You can then replicate the classified ads by imitating them and selling the same product. If you see many advertisements for information on loosing weight you know that there is a become market among the readers for weight loss products. Capitalize on that knowledge by putting together your own weight loss information. The information is as easy to obtain as go to the library and reading some of the weight loss books on the shelves. You then copy some of your favorite ideas and package them into your own information booklet. You are now ready to sell your own information booklet on loosing weight.

Always try to advertise in the highest circulation publications even if the cost is higher. The higher cost will be worth it when the orders start flowing in. While there are hundreds of small shopper papers with cheap classified ad rates, I would give it some serious thought before using them. They seem attractive because they offer rates of as low as .25 a word. But they are cheap for a reason so beware. On the other hand since you probably will be one of the few advertisers in the shopper newspaper you will, not have any competition from the other classified ads. I sure would love to receive a letter from a Mail Order entrepreneur telling me how he has built a fortune using low circulation publications. You might be the first one if your ad is innovative and special enough.

The most effective classified ad strategy requires the Mail Order advertiser to place ads in different publications and keep track of the response rate for each ad. This way you will know which ads are pulling in the most responses. You should use different department numbers on each ad so you will be able to determine from which ad the response came from. You also want to be able to keep track of which publication brings in the most responses so you can concentrate your classified ad campaign in that publication. An advanced Mail Or5dfer operator would then proceed to test a few different ads in the best performing publication. The Mail Order operator will then know which ad brings in the highest response rate. Once you discover the ad that brings in the highest response rate you should repeat that ad for as long as it continues bringing in orders. An effective classified ad can continue to bring in sales for years.

The writing of the classified ad will have the highest affect on its success. The ad should be written with the buyer in mind. By this I mean that you should place yourself in the shoes of the buyer and decide what it is that the buyer would need to read to encourage him to respond. What are the key words that would make you as a buyer respond to the ad?

I bet some words that would make you look twice are Free, $1,000,000, Wealthy, Millionaire, Fast, Rich, Business, Profit and How to. There are many other key words that will catch someone's interest because of what they promise. When you see the word Free you know that you can receive something without having to spend nay money. When you see the sum 1,000,000, or when you read the words Rich, Millionaire, Rich, you start to think of how you can become rich. Everyone in life wants solutions for improving their financial and physical condition. You need to use key words that hold the promise of helping people improve their lives. They will then respond in droves to the promise of becoming rich beyond their wildest dreams. Make sure that if you offer to help someone become rich that you can deliver by offering sound advice that they can use to make money.

The first two words of a classified ad are usually highlighted by the publication to make the ad more noticeable. You want to make sure that those two words will grab people's attention when they look at them. This is your opportunity to use the words that will make your potential buyer become excited sand rush to place an order from your classified ad. The rest of the ad must continue to hold their interest by making a strong claim that promises to fulfill their needs. If the need of your buyer is to make more money then the classified ad has to offer to show them hot to make money. If your buyers want to learn how to paint the ad must say something like "Learn how to paint like a pro". Since they want to learn how to paint and they want to become good painters your ad has to tell them that they will learn how to paint like experts. Everyone wants to learn how to achieve and succeed in his or her preferred hobby so you need to tell people that your information is what will help them achieve that goal. People buy because they are looking to fulfill a need so you need to word your classified as so people will realize that their need is going to be met.

The last part of your classified ad is where you convince the reader to place an order. You need to use the last few words of the ad to remove any doubts and further stimulate the prospect into action. Be imaginative and you can produce classified ads that will generate thousands of dollars in orders.

Here is a great sample of an effective ad

Instant Wealth through Mail Order

Send $5 Legacy 44 His St New York NY 10022

The ad is straight to the point and catches people's attention. It tells people that if they place an order they will learn how to instantly make money by operating Mail Order business. Two important needs are met with the ad, the desire to make money and the desire to make money fast. The ad can also start out with the words Become Rich, since this phrase would also fulfill the desire of people to become rich. Keep in mind that you will want to offer genuine information because you want your customers to remain happy so they will order again from you. I have written a few books and always make sure that my readers can benefit from the information. I know that my success depends on my readers being able to succeed with the information that I have given them. If I help someone with one of my books I know that he or she will want to buy mo other books. You need to take the same attitude, if you want to have repeat customers you need to do a professional job of writing your booklets and catalogs and always offer genuine information that can help people reach their goals.

CONCLUSION

I hope you enjoyed this book and that it inspired you to start your own Mail Order business. I want to take this opportunity to urge you to act on your plans. Now that you have finished the book you are excited because you have read how to make millions of dollars in your Mail Order business. This excitement is genuine because this book contains enough information to help any aspiring entrepreneur succeed in one of the most lucrative businesses in the world. Your entire costs for starting the business is minimal and the rewards that the business can produce are unlimited. This is your opportunity to never to have live paycheck to paycheck again. Instead of being obedient to the desires of others you can take your life into your own hands and build your own fortune as s elf employed individual. I believe in your ability to succeed in your business and I look forward to hearing from you.

This is not an easy business and it will require time and effort. But if you put in the time and effort and follow the advice contained in this book you will be on your way to becoming rich. Apply the information in this book starting today and you will be on your way to prospering tomorrow. I hope to hear from you,

Sincerely,
Donny Lowy
legacytrader@aol.com

Printed in the United States
701900002B

9 780738 856292